GIVE ME STRENGTH
BALANCE
AND BONE
EXERCISES FOR SENIORS
AN ILLUSTRATED GUIDE TO PREVENT FALLING

INCLUDES VIDEO LINKS TO THE EXERCISES

Basic At-Home Workouts to Improve Posture, Strengthen Bone Density, and Fight Osteoporosis.

BY MATTHEW CASE

SMC MEDIA LLC

SEMPER DOCTRINA

A FREE GIFT FOR YOU!

Before you begin this book, please take advantage of the **5 Free Bonuses** from the **Give Me Strength Quick Start Guide**. Inside this guide, you will receive:

Free Bonus #1 - Dancing for Strength Bonus Workout

In this bonus workout, you'll see additional core and balance exercises and a special "Dancing for Strength" workout. It will feature a weblink to a custom music playlist to give you additional "pep in your step" while you exercise.

Free Bonus #2 - 5x5 Fitness Challenge

This freebie will provide you with a quick roadmap for establishing motivation, goals, and much more. I encourage you to complete this 5x5 Fitness Challenge. Complete 1 challenge per day for a total of 5 in 5 days! See Free Bonus #3 for the companion piece to this.

Free Bonus #3 - Transformation Tools

These tools are useful for the 5 x 5 Fitness Challenge. They include; 5 whys, 5 fitness goals, 5 ways to better sleep, 5 hints to stay hydrated, and 5 tips to improve your thought life. They are easy to print, use and share with others.

Free Bonus #4 - Workout Calendar

This fantastic freebie is a calendar template that you can use to track your workouts during the month. It's easy to get off track, but this calendar will help you plan the month and showcase all your hard work done!

Free Bonus #5 - Give Me Strength Recipes, Shopping List

This bonus provides five tasty recipes for a fit lifestyle. It also contains a shopping list and offers healthy suggestions for grocery shopping. Good nutrition is key to successful balance training.

To receive your 5 free bonuses, scan this QR code:

LEAVE A QUICK REVIEW

I would be incredibly grateful if you would please take 30 seconds to write a brief review, even if it's just a few sentences. Visit this webpage to leave a quick review: www.givemestrengthfitness.com/review2 or **scan this QR code:**

Table of Contents

INTRODUCTION

"Beautiful young people are accidents of nature,
but beautiful old people are works of art."
– Eleanor Roosevelt

———

Once there was a lavish cruise ship that accommodated thousands of people. Its sophisticated design and services made it one of the most famous cruise ships in the world. Then one day, the engine failed, and no one could figure out why.

One high-tech mechanic after another tried their hands at fixing the engine, but none could get it to work. Finally, after months at the harbor and the company quickly losing money every second the ship was at the dock, they were hard-pressed to bite the bullet and replace the engine. But they wanted to try every professional first.

And so, they brought in a retired man who had been working on ships since he was a child. He showed up carrying a massive bag of tools. He asked for the location and went straight to work. This professional was meticulous with his work and examined every inch of the engine.

Two of the company owners watched the man with bated breath, praying that their problem would be resolved soon and the ship would be seaworthy once more. After going over the engine, the man reached into his toolbox and pulled out a comically small hammer. He tapped a few spots a couple of times and started the engine.

Surprisingly, it roared to life. The whole thing took less than 30 minutes. The owners were very impressed and told the old man to invoice them for his service. They then parted ways.

A week after, the owners received an invoice from the old man. The price: $50,000.

"What?! This charge is daylight robbery!" one of the owners said. They then wrote to the man asking him to itemize his invoice. It arrived in the mail, and it read:

Hourly rate: $18
Tapping with a hammer: $2
Knowing where to tap: $49,980

So how is this story relevant? Well, there are a couple of things we could learn from this.

For one, no matter your current problems, the solution is often straightforward. Life is complicated, so there is no point in making things even more complex than they must be.

Also, it takes a lot of effort for someone to do something effortlessly. You may admire some athletes or famous people who can perform difficult feats without a sweat. What a lot of people do not see is the countless hours they spent behind the scenes practicing. They only got so good at doing something perfectly and effortlessly because they spent countless hours doing something badly.

So, how does any of this play into health? If I had to guess, you are either having health problems or doing your best to avoid them. You may have talked with many doctors – professionals – and got very little from all that time. Maybe you have tried many things you saw online already, but nothing worked for you.

The reality is that the solution to your problems, at least as far as your bones and balance are concerned, is simpler than you think! All it takes is a few taps in the right places.

Aging is an inevitable part of life. Everybody has to deal with it at some point. By that, I mean everybody, even the people you may admire. Gwyneth Paltrow, Britt Eckland, and Sally Field have osteoporosis. George W. Bush, Harrison Ford, and Usain Bolt deal with chronic back pain. Aging does not discriminate, so you are not alone here. But just because everybody is dealing with it does not mean you can afford to be complacent.

Numbers Don't Lie

Every year, over 300,000 people over 65 seek hospitalization for hip fractures. Unfortunately, over 95% of those cases were caused by falling, and 75% of the patients were women. Even worse, your chance of breaking your hip increases as you age. Hip fractures are preventable through various means, but arguably the best and most effective solution is to take up strength training and balance exercises. Why?

Aging is a natural part of life, so you can do nothing about it, right? Wrong! There are many ways to minimize the effect of aging, and your balance is no exception.

As people age, their balance tends to deteriorate, but this problem is not exclusive to older adults. Balance, in general, helps prevent injury. Younger people with excellent balance usually perform better at various activities than those without. Plus, the first group's risk for accidents and injury is also lower.

Balance is one of those skills that become more important as you age. You need to maintain it, or you lose it. While younger people can take a fall just fine, the effect can be devasting among seniors. Harvard Medical School pointed out that balance training goes a long way in reducing the risk of falls in older adults. Other benefits include:

- Better reaction: A faster reaction time might save you from a fall, and you can improve that through exercise and balance training.
- Improved muscle tone: You will have better balance overall. Even if you fall, your muscles will provide more cushion to protect your bones.
- Bone strength: Exercise and resistance training improves bone strength, making us less likely to fracture if we fall.
- Cognitive ability: Simply put, your mind will be sharper, and your coordination will improve.

Is Ignorance Really Bliss?

Now, some of you might wonder if you can just forgo all this passionate, data-driven material. I mean, you can, and there is not much I can do to force you to work out. And perhaps the benefits of exercise and balance training are not convincing enough to compel you to change your lifestyle. So, let's "flip the script" then and see what risks you may face if you ignore all of this.

The benefits of exercising are clear. Everybody knows an active lifestyle is best for one's health, so why isn't everybody hitting the gym (or home gym), especially the seniors?

There are many reasons why that is the case. Some seniors think that a gym membership is too expensive or that transportation to one is inconvenient. Plus, they may have chronic health conditions that make exercise challenging. Whatever the reason may be, the result remains the same. The lack of exercise will lead to an overall decline in health.

Just like the benefits of an active lifestyle, the risks of a sedentary lifestyle are also well-known. They are especially severe among seniors, however. The risks include:

- Loss of bone density
- Loss of muscle mass
- Increased frailty
- Higher risks of falls and injuries
- Higher risk for chronic conditions such as depression, obesity, diabetes, and heart disease

How to Use This Book

This book has two parts. Part one, consisting of chapters 1 to 7, explains the fundamentals: who, what, and why. There, I will tell you where to tap away at your problems. Part two, covering chapters 8 and 9, delves into exercises and workouts, providing the tools and guidance for action. There, we will discuss various exercises and workouts – the hammer with which to tap, the where, when, and how.

You might wonder why there are seven chapters on research and lifestyle data before diving into exercises. The truth is, addressing balance and bone issues requires more than just mobility exercises. While balance exercises are crucial, understanding how your balance and bones work and how to prepare for exercise is equally important. This book emphasizes how to achieve a better overall balanced lifestyle rather than mere adjustments to our routines.

For beginners, acquiring basic knowledge is vital. Hence, the initial part of the book is filled with data and clear explanations. Knowing the "why" helps you better implement the "how," and understanding the benefits reinforces your commitment to new lifestyle choices.

Of course, if you prefer immediate action, you can jump straight to part two and begin right away. Then, you can always return to part one for further knowledge if desired.

Regardless of your chosen path, I encourage you to explore the mechanics of good balance and the impact of bone health. The first part also covers essential factors like nutrition, hydration, breathing, and sleep, as they significantly contribute to bone strength and balance improvement. I'd be remiss if I didn't include this information.

About the Author

This project all started with my mother, Nancy. In 2018, she was already struggling with some back and leg pain while she was moving to a smaller house. The move took a toll on her body and while she pushed through it, her pain became unbearable in the weeks and months to come. She needed to take action.

Consultations with various specialists proved fruitless save for the promise of relief by using drugs and invasive surgeries, which frightened her. So instead, after extensive research, she took a risk and bravely decided to turn toward some natural alternatives including strength and balance workouts.

Through more research, nutrition changes, and consistent exercise my mom made a complete recovery, and I was there to witness it all. She slept better, walked without assistance, lost weight, had less anxiety, and her back and leg pain vanished. She was a new woman.

While she's shared her personal progress with a small group of friends and family, I thought it needed a bigger platform. After seeing her amazing recovery first hand, I wanted to share a slice of her story and what she learned with others.

Moreover, I am in my 50s, and I believe I speak for everybody here that no one wants to deal with back and other aging-related pains. A top priority for me is to stay healthy for my family, especially seeing what she went through. So I decided to dive in with two feet, to learn what she learned and take it one step further…write a book about it.

As for me, my history and love for fitness and health runs deep. I am an athlete and the son of a coach and teacher. I've always wanted (and needed) to understand how the human body works. I was an All-American wrestler at Northwestern University, a team captain, and a recipient of the Big Ten Medal of Honor. I've trained alongside NCAA, Olympic and World Champion athletes and I've coached at many different levels.

But what really inspired me to write this book didn't come from my athletic background. It came from my mom. And while she is a world-class mom, she is no world-class athlete. She is simply an average senior who was trying to get by each day without pain. Her journey toward recovery is one of hope, which I would like to give you in these pages.

For the record, this book will not be laying out how to train like an elite athlete. I am not going to show you that the only way to regain your balance and bone strength is through intense 3-hour workouts. Instead, I will offer you simple, practical, field-tested, science-based approaches to building balance, strength, and energy so you can avoid injuries. I will tell you how to regain your agility and vitality through realistic balance, bone, and posture workouts. And I will tell you exactly where and how to tap with that little hammer.

Of course, my words are not gospel, and I do not claim to have the holy grail of lasting youth. All I have to share is the knowledge I've accumulated while working with athletes, my personal research, and what my mother has passed on to me.

So, as per my mom's story there is still hope. There is still time. You can still reclaim your strength, eliminate pain and stand tall once more. You can still be energetic and better balanced. We will work together and help you reclaim your youth in this book.

Let's get started!

PART ONE

UNDERSTANDING BALANCE & BONES

1

BALANCE AND BONES
SETTING THE STAGE

*"Age is just a number. It's totally irrelevant unless, of course,
you happen to be a bottle of wine."*
– Joan Collins

———

It is no secret that most of our physical health systems deteriorate as we age. Our balance and bones, which work together more closely than we realize, are no exceptions. Consequently, our quality of life can decline in many areas if we are not diligent to maintain them. These systems can include, but are not limited to:

Cardiovascular system: your arteries and blood vessels can become stiffer. That means your heart muscles work harder to push blood throughout your body. This effect is barely noticeable because your resting heart rate remains the same. However, this effect sticks out when you start to do strenuous activities, as your heart rate may not get as high as it once did.

Your bones and muscles: they may become more fragile. Muscles can lose strength, and bones are more susceptible to fracture. These may affect your stability, balance, and coordination.

Your joints and cartilage: our cartilage may become thinner, the synovial fluids inside the joints decrease, and the ligaments shorten, resulting in less flexible joint movements.

Digestive system: the structure in your large intestine can change as you age, resulting in constipation. But this condition can also be caused by a lack of water, exercise, and fiber. Other contributing factors include other health conditions like diabetes and medication.

Cognition: simply put, you might suffer from a "foggy brain." Some words or even names might slip by you. The most common sign is the difficulty in multitasking.

So, these declining systems are the bad news about aging. As we peel back this onion, it all sounds a bit grim, doesn't it. Is there any good news in all this? Absolutely!

Fine Wine or "Two Buck Chuck"?

First, you must understand that your body's systems do not have to be affected the way that the "decline" is described. Yes, our bodies inevitably start their aging processes, which most people start to see and feel in their 50s. However, this does not mean there isn't anything we can do about it. You and I absolutely have the power to change our aging trajectory and future health. It simply boils down to a decision. A decision to either age like a fine wine or, a Two-Buck Chuck.

Now, I'm guessing that you have heard the phrase regarding how someone has "aged like a fine wine." And I'm also guessing that you've either had your fair share of Two-Buck Chucks or, you've at least heard of the brand name, Charles Shaw wines aka Two-Buck-Chuck. Yes? If you haven't then please let me explain.

Almost anyone who has tasted both fine or "not so fine wine" can usually tell the difference and, if offered a free glass of each, would usually choose the fine wine. Sure, a bottle Two-Buck Chuck costs about "2 bucks" and is a bargain for frugal consumers like me. However, you can really only drink them shortly after buying them and they often taste a bit bitter and acidic. Conversely, fine wine only gets better with age, and the flavors and levels of smoothness can be otherworldly.

You're probably already aware that the difference between a fine wine and a two-buck chuck lies in the process. Quality wine comes from better grapes, barrels, and processing methods. Sure, it takes a lot more time and effort to make good wine (hence the higher price), but your pallet should tell you that it is more than worth it.

What my rough analogy is saying here is that similar to the vintners who produce the wine, whether we age like a Two-Buck Chuck or a fine wine is entirely up to us. It's our decision. We have complete control over our "inner grapes" and how we process them. So, our bodies can either become that fine expensive wine that gets better with age by processing our grapes well, or we can become complacent, cheap, and yes…even slightly bitter.

Keeping Hope Alive

As you are reading this, you might be hit with a sense of worry or fear. Or, at the very least, you might be mildly concerned about aging. The process of discovery here isn't all unicorns and rainbows. But whichever part of the "concerned spectrum" you fall on, the human body is much more resilient than you think. Using another quick analogy, a car engine with 100,000 miles can still run better than one with 1,000 miles. What is the secret? Two words…proper maintenance.

The same also applies to us. More specifically, our bones and muscles. Yes, as we've stated, our bodies will deteriorate as we age. But there is hope and lots of it! There are many ways to combat aging and improve our quality of life. In fact, if you follow everything we cover in this book, you might even become more fit and more flexible than those in their 30s or even 20s!

Even so, seeing and feeling your body deteriorating as you age can be disheartening. For this reason, it is vital to maintain a positive outlook. Now, one can be forgiven for assuming that optimism will not fix that back pain. But, in reality, it can!

You probably already know what the problems are, and I will give you the tools for the job. That way, just like that repairman who earned millions with a tap of a hammer, you can turn your life around by following the activities highlighted in this book. Hope itself will be your starting point in regaining and retaining your agility and balance as a senior. From there, you just need the know "how."

According to Harvard University's Institute for Quantitative Social Science study, hope is critical for senior mental health. The study involved around 13,000 U.S. adults over 50 years old. Researchers found that optimistic people also had better health and reduced risk of various health conditions. Not to mention, being positive in general is also beneficial for your mental health.

Fun fact: Stress can actually cause back pain. Don't believe me? Ask your doctor. Another reason to stay positive, right?

Benefits of Exercise

There are not many, but there are a sadistic few who exercise because the activity can be painful and tiring. I am not one of them. The baffling fact is that although working out can sometimes make you feel a bit terrible in that moment or even that next day, if you push through it will enable you to feel incredible over time. Similarly, even though you might feel nice and comfy in the moment as a consistent couch potato, it will only worsen your mental and physical health. Exercising, despite the obstacles, will yield countless benefits, including:

Better Mood

Exercise helps improve our moods and combats negative emotions, keeping anxiety, depression, and stress at bay. This results from the changes in a part of our brain that controls stress and anxiety. Going active can also heighten brain sensitivity to noradrenaline (a neurotransmitter and hormone) and serotonin – hormones that fight feelings and depression. Moreover, exercising can also produce endorphins, which help us feel better and reduce our perception of pain.

What is fascinating is that it really does not matter what workouts we do. So long as you are active, no matter what the activity or intensity is, you will start to feel better. This benefit is so powerful that you will notice it even in the short run, in as little as 1-2 weeks.

Weight Loss

To fully appreciate how exercise leads to weight loss, we must understand the relationship between energy expenditure and exercise. You may often hear that weight loss is a simple equation between energy intake through eating and energy expenditure. You see, your body burns through energy in 3 main ways:

- Breaking down (digesting) food
- Exercising
- Maintaining bodily functions

The theory is that you can induce weight loss through calorie deficit – where the energy intake is lower than the energy expenditure. So, you can either eat less or be more active. The second alternative is more practical because you must eat something eventually.

Though you might associate working out with youths, the truth is that there are a ton of exercises suitable for seniors. The only real difference comes down to intensity levels. But, as I mentioned before, studies suggest that your mood will improve just by working out, regardless of the intensity.

Plus, research also shows that a combination of resistance (strength training) and aerobic exercises (conditioning) is effective in maintaining muscle mass while also maximizing fat loss.

Strengthens Bones and Muscles

You must work your bones and muscles to maintain their functionality and resilience. For this, exercise is also essential. As we age, we usually lose muscle mass and function, both of which contribute to the risk of injury. So, regular physical activities go a long way in minimizing muscle loss and maintaining muscle strength.

Elevates Your Energy Levels

As mentioned, exercises can tire us out in the moment, yet they are huge energy boosters over time. They work wonders in keeping the feelings of fatigue at bay. Another significant benefit is that exercising also improves our heart and lung health, both of which play a huge role in determining our energy levels.

The more we move, the more oxygen is delivered to our muscles as our heart pumps more blood. So through regular exercising, our heart becomes more efficient. That means it can better deliver oxygen throughout our body, which also helps our muscles be more efficient.

You may find yourself going out of breath during strenuous activities at first. However, if you maintain your workout routine for a while, those activities start to become less tiring. This result is thanks to the improved efficiency of both our hearts and lungs, so we need less energy to do the same thing.

Combats Chronic Diseases

The lack of regular physical activity is a primary cause of various chronic diseases. Regular exercise lowers blood pressure and cholesterol levels and improves heart health, body composition, and insulin sensitivity. These benefits prevent chronic conditions such as type 2 diabetes, heart disease, hypertension, and cancer.

Better Quality of Life
Other benefits include:

- Better sleep quality: When we burn all that extra energy throughout the day, we fall asleep more easily.
- Less pain: Recent studies show that exercise can relieve chronic pain and raise pain tolerance.
- Improved skin health: Oxidative stress can powerfully affect our skin. Regular moderate exercise helps the body produce natural antioxidants, protecting cells against oxidative stress. Plus, exercise stimulates blood flow and can help delay the appearance of skin aging.

Dangers of Not Exercising

On the other end of the spectrum, what dangers await us if we continue to lead a sedentary lifestyle? The unfortunate truth is that we need to keep exercising. When we stop, "detraining" occurs. It is where our bodies quickly lose the positive benefits of working out. So, what can happen if we quit?

Muscle Atrophy
When we work out, we maintain muscle mass, maintaining its strength. When we stop, major muscle groups start to deteriorate. It takes around two weeks for this to start. With weak muscles comes weak bones as well. Weak muscles cannot exert enough pressure on bones to stimulate growth.

Worse Moods
Given how exercise elevates our mood, the opposite is also true. We will experience more intense fatigue and negative feelings if we stop exercising. This results from the endorphin we usually get from working out. Without it, we could face a higher risk of depression, anxiety, loneliness, etc.

Higher Risk for Various Health Conditions

Living a sedentary lifestyle puts us at risk of many health problems, such as type 2 diabetes, cardiovascular diseases, hypertension, etc. This problem applies to all ages, but the risk is even greater among seniors.

Why Good Nutrition?

Of course, it takes a bit more than working out to combat aging. Maintaining a good diet also goes a long way because it does the job differently than working out. Though we will dive deeply into how nutrition helps your health and balance overall, I would like to briefly review how vital nutrition is.

- Bone health: We understand how essential bones are to one's overall balance. Though they may seem rigid, they can change based on your lifestyle and what you feed them. They have tiny cracks and damage as you go about your day. They can adapt, repair, and strengthen with proper nutrition (vitamin D, protein, phosphorus, sodium, magnesium, calcium, etc.). However, if you feed them the wrong things, your bones cannot recover as well, if at all.
- Gut health: When discussing food, we must examine where food is processed. Our guts also contribute much to our overall balance by supporting bone health. For this, we have the gut microbiota (a diverse community of bacteria and other microbes living in your gastrointestinal tract, especially the large intestine) to thank. One byproduct of their fermentation is short-chain fatty acids which allow our bodies to absorb more calcium, magnesium, and other minerals. In other words, our bodies can acquire more materials to repair and strengthen our bones.

Balance and Bones Are Critical

To maintain an active lifestyle as we age, we need to keep our balance. Balance declines as we age, thanks to the loss of muscle mass and bone density, among other things. The CDC released some interesting numbers:

- 1 out of 4 seniors suffers from a fall every year, but fewer than half of them tell their doctor.
- Your likelihood of falling doubles after the first fall.
- 1 out of 5 falls leads to severe injuries such as head injury and broken bones.

- 3 million cases in the emergency department are caused by falls every year.
- Over 800,000 patients are hospitalized because of a fall injury annually.
- The problem with falls is that it is a self-perpetuating cycle. A sedentary lifestyle compromises the bones and muscles, weakening one's balance and leading to falls and injuries. These injuries can make it difficult for a person to get around on their own. This is a problem for many reasons:
- Falls can cause broken bones such as arm, wrist, ankle, and hip fractures.
- Falls can also cause serious head injuries.
- Those who fall can develop a fear of falling, so they try to move as little as possible. The lack of activities further weakens the bones and muscles, increasing the likelihood of falling.

Chapter Summary

- Our body deteriorates as we age. It is a natural process, but there are ways to slow aging. All it takes is some know-how.
- The benefits of an active lifestyle are apparent. We will feel stronger, better, more energetic, and healthier overall.
- On the flip side, a sedentary lifestyle, though seemingly comfortable initially, can be detrimental and even fatal.
- What we eat also plays a significant role in balance as well. Our bones, muscles, and body as a whole can only get as healthy as the foods we eat.
- Falls can be devastating for seniors due to loss of muscle mass and weaker bones. Even worse still, injuries caused by falls hinder one's ability to move around, which means more difficulty transitioning to an active lifestyle. So, it is always best to start early.

2

STRIKING A GOOD BALANCE

"Life is like riding a bicycle. To keep your balance, you must keep moving."
– Albert Einstein.

———

We have covered some benefits of having a good balance, but what it can offer you goes much deeper. And so, this chapter serves as a deep dive into what good things await you when you start making lifestyle changes.

A Critical Balance Test

A study published in the British Journal of Sports Medicine proposed an exciting metric to determine whether you have a good balance. Try to stand on one leg for about 10 seconds. It is a straightforward test that accesses various systems in your body. The study suggested that those who cannot pass this test have a twice higher risk of death within the next decade. <u>You may want to reread that last sentence.</u>

This study involved 1,702 people, and the average age was 61. Two-thirds of them were men. Around 20% of the participants failed the test. Researchers followed these participants for the next seven years, during which 123 people died. So, 7% of the participants died within ten years after the test. What was interesting was the proportion of deaths. Among those who failed the test, 17.5% passed away, compared to only 4.5% of those who did pass the test.

To be precise, those who could not complete the test had an 84% higher risk of death from any cause. This still applies when you consider other factors such as preexisting conditions, BMI, gender, age, and other factors.

While the study failed to consider things such as a history of falls, pattern of physical activity, diet, smoking, etc., exercise is a pretty good indicator of one's health. So, if someone cannot perform that 10-second stand, they probably need to reflect on their health risks.

Another study in 2017 suggested that balance training can improve our memory and spatial cognition, which is a process that involves how our brain organizes and uses information about its environment. Here, researchers examined 70 healthy individuals in Germany. They were not athletes with excellent balance, however. So, researchers put these individuals into two groups. One went through a balance training program, and the other did not. Both groups went through a test for memory and spatial cognition before and after the training program.

The result was predictable – the first group performed much better after participating in the program.

Of course, such studies were relatively short-term, and it is challenging to draw long-term conclusions. However, these studies and many others on similar subjects give us a glimpse into the myriad health benefits of balance exercises. They are suitable for our brains.

These exercises make use of an interesting mechanic called neuroplasticity. The brain can change its neural pathways based on growth and reorganization. This same process is how we learn a new language, how to drive, and how to play the guitar. Balance training also utilizes this neuroplasticity.

Many people think that balance is more than just how long we can stand on one leg. According to Dr. Anat Lubetzky, Ph.D., associate professor of physical therapy at New York University, falls do not occur because they cannot maintain their position. You don't just stand firmly on two feet and suddenly fall unless a severe medical condition happens. Instead, people fall when the environment changes, so balance is much more complex than most think.

In other words, balancing exercise involves more than just standing on one leg. The Scientific Reports study used a dynamic balance training program where participants were asked to stand on one leg while being pulled with an elastic strap and stand on a wobbling board while passing a medicine ball to another person. Such exercises engage your coordination, planning, thinking, and reaction. Because they are more complex, they also engage the brain more.

It is worth keeping in mind that any exercise is better than none. Dr. Lubetzky says that any exercise is good for our brain. Just because you cannot do a triple somersault on a wobbly skateboard does not mean you should forgo exercise. Some milder activities can still do our brain a lot of good. Dr. Kilgore, MD, a neurologist based in California, believes cardiovascular exercise is excellent because it improves the efficiency of our lungs and heart.

How does this benefit the brain? Well, because the brain requires blood and oxygen to function, the efficiency in our lungs and heart ensure that our brain is getting as much nutrients and oxygen as it needs to function optimally. As a result, both cardiovascular and strength training help stave off dementia.

Components of Balance

As mentioned before, balance is complex. It involves information from:

- Visual system: Our eyes help us see where we are in the environment around us.
- Proprioceptive input: Our muscles, tendons, and joints help you understand our body's placement in the environment.
- Vestibular system: The balance organs inside the inner ear tell the brain about the movement and position of the head. That way, the brain knows whether the head is upright and stationary or not.

The brain stem puts all this information together, with help from other parts of the brain, to help us navigate the world. Our brains then send messages to various body parts to help us maintain balance as we move from point A to point B.

Our bones and muscles also play a massive role in this delicate system of balance – more than just keeping our body structurally sound. For example, the joint cannot move well if our muscles are weak or not sufficiently flexible. Maybe it will be jerky, or you cannot engage in a full range of motion. All of these cause balance problems.

Many older adults suffer from muscle mass loss or strength despite the mass staying constant. Both conditions result in weak muscles, and they would be unable to move joints as they are supposed to. As a result, it takes time to quickly adjust and maintain balance which can lead to falls.

Some senior adults can also struggle with a loss of bone density. Simply put, this means our bones are fragile, and we can lose both flexibility and strength if we have limited mobility because of a fracture. This, too, can put our long-term balance at risk.

Moreover, our musculoskeletal system also affects our overall balance. It is a combination of bones, cartilage, ligaments, tendons, and connective tissues. Your skeleton gives a framework for all of them. Together, they support our body's posture and weight and allow us to move around.

Movements occur when our brain sends a message to activate our skeletal muscles. The muscle fibers then contract in response, which pulls on the tendons. These tendons then pull on the bone, moving it. Our brain also sends another message to contract the muscles, allowing the bones to come to a resting position.

Balance or lack thereof comes from the need for coordination in any part of this system. The brain may not effectively send signals to the muscles. The muscles may lack the mass or strength to pull on the tendons, and the tendons may wear down so they cannot pull on the bones with the same amount of force, etc.

All of these problems compromise the body's coordination, which is usually how falls occur. Falls do not happen because you cannot stand on one foot. They occur because our body does not coordinate and function as it should.

How Balance Unbalances

Most people develop balance problems as they age. This is because every component of our balance system starts to deteriorate. For example, as our eyesight worsens, our brain's ability to send signals to the body also worsens, and our strength also declines. Other than the apparent reasons for balance problems, such as alcohol and medications, many other factors can cause them, such as:

- Inner ear: The labyrinth in the inner ear is responsible for balance. When it is inflamed, we may experience imbalance and vertigo. Ear infections and diseases can also lead to labyrinthitis.
- Cardiovascular disease: Abnormal heart rhythms, blocked or narrowed blood vessels, lowering blood volume, or thickened heart muscle can all cause lightheadedness.
- Nerve damage
- Joint, muscle, or vision problems: Weak muscles and unstable joints can contribute to loss of balance. Eyesight problems can also cause instability.
- Anxiety and other psychiatric disorders can also cause dizziness.

Balancing the Consequences

What happens when we have balance impairment?

- Limited participation in functional activities, causing decreased strength, range of motion, and endurance.
- While judgment, attention, memory, and cognition deficits contribute to balance deficits, they also hinder the learning process needed to reestablish balance skills.
- Other symptoms: Dizziness, hearing impairment, vertigo, unsteady gait, visual impairment, restricted movement due to fear of falls, reliance on arms and hands for support, impaired postural control, etc.

Balancing the Equation

With this in mind, how can we improve our balance? While our balance tends to decline with age, we can do many things to regain our agility.

Get Moving

While it is true that the loss of mobility results from aging – a completely natural process – that does not mean we should sit there and take it. When people start losing their balance, many try to move around as little as possible. Unfortunately, this will only lead to a worse balance over time.

Instead, get off the couch and get active. We only need to do a little at this early stage. Go for a walk or a light jog and enjoy it. Just a 10-minute walk will do our bodies a lot of good. The point is to have fun getting active again and stick to what is comfortable. Just start slow and have fun.

Balance Exercises

You can start doing specific balance exercises when you are comfortable moving around again. We will cover this in detail in chapters 8 and 9. The foremost thing you need to remember here is quality over quantity. What is important here is not repetition but form. Having the perfect form means engaging the right muscles and going through the proper range of motion for the best results. An imperfect form can increase your risk of injury, so focus on getting the proper form first.

Changing Your Focus

Where we focus can also improve or hinder our balance. Research shows that when we concentrate on a point outside our body, our balance improves during movement and while stationary. For example, when doing an exercise, instead of focusing on the activity or your feet, try to focus on something at least 10 feet away from you. In doing so, your body will go on autopilot mode and complete the repetition without any conscious inputs from your brain.

Keep at It

As mentioned, our muscles, bones, and overall balance will deteriorate when we no longer exercise. So, it would be best if we kept at it. Consider going for walks, biking, or taking the stairs when the opportunity presents itself. Yoga and tai chi also do wonders in working our muscles and working our balancing skills.

Positive Effects of Balance Exercises

One study completed by Nagy et al. found that an 8-week program that combined flexibility, strength, and aerobic exercises helped improve the postural control of older adults. Other aspects of quality-of-life improvements from balance exercise include:

- Improved cognitive performance.
- Combats the fear of falling.
- Improved cognitive functions.

- Better static and dynamic balance and strength

Stretching Helps Balance

A study published by PubMed Central showed that stretches affect both peripheral neural and mechanical output. These changes allow the body to adapt to stability challenges. In addition, stretching can reduce the stiffness of the joints, allowing better movement. A 30-second stretching regimen is most effective since going any longer has no extra benefit.

Posture and Balance

Just by reading the subtitle, you might sit straight already. However, our posture does affect our balance because our body must work harder if the spine is out of its normal alignment. It is a lot easier to balance a broomstick when it is upright, after all. Good posture has many benefits, such as:

- Better mood: Standing straight and tall will give us that extra boost in your confidence.
- Better bone, joint, and muscle health: good posture puts less strain on our bones and muscles.
- Better breathing: good posture also puts less pressure on the diaphragm, which enables us to breathe deeply and clearly.
- Infrequent headache: Bad posture puts extra strain on the shoulders, leading to headaches.
- Stronger core and back muscles: good posture engages those muscles, improving our stability and balance.
- Better range of motion: good posture results in more balanced musculature, enabling a better range of motion.
- Prevents injury: better strength and flexibility enable correct lifting techniques, resulting in a lower chance of injury.
- Less fatigue: Proper posture means less muscular imbalance in the body so that we can move more efficiently.

Personal At-Home Balance Assessment

If you are curious, there are ways to see how good your balance is without seeing a specialist. Though the pros can give you a much more detailed understanding of how your body performs, you can get a good idea by doing some tests at home.

One method is the 10-second test we mentioned before. All you have to do is stand on one leg and see if you can maintain your balance for 10 seconds. Just make sure to have a chair or rail nearby to be safe.

Another technique is to stand with your feet together, with the ankles touching. Fold your arms across your chest. Then, close your eyes and stand still for a minute. You might sway a bit, and that is fine.

A third method is to put one foot right before the other and close your eyes. Your balance is good if you can maintain this position for 30 seconds on both sides.

These are a few easy at-home assessments you can do at home. But, again, do this with someone nearby or with something to grab quickly in case you lose your balance.

Chapter Summary
- Good balance has many benefits for one's quality of life, such as longevity, confidence, higher cognitive abilities, etc.
- Good balance requires coordination from various systems in the body, such as the muscles, bones, eyes, inner ear, and the brain, to manage everything. If any component in this complex system is not functioning correctly, your balance will be compromised.
- Although aging is a primary factor contributing to a loss of balance, many health conditions affect various components of our balance, such as loss of muscle mass, fragile bones, cardiovascular problems, etc.
- Balance is a severe issue among seniors. While adults and teens can take a fall with grace, statistics show they can be devastating among seniors.
- Fortunately, improving one's balance is a matter of getting active again. You can go at your speed and give yourself a while to get comfortable with this new lifestyle. From there, you can try the exercises in this book to help you regain your balance and agility.

3

BONING UP ON BONES

"To succeed in life, you need three things: a wishbone, a backbone, and a funny bone!"
– Reba McEntire

———

Many of us are already familiar with bones' key role in our bodies. However, your bones are much more than support beams for your organs. This chapter will discuss why our bones are much more important than you think and will give us steps on how to improve them.

The Significance of Bones

What are Our Bones' Functions?

Bones are essential for our skeletal system, being both lightweight and incredibly strong. Surprisingly, adults have 206 bones on average, although we initially start with over 300. What happens to the rest? Oddly enough, they fuse together as we grow. These unified bones work together to perform a multitude of functions in our bodies, such as:

- Support our body and help us move: Our bones hold up our body. Without them, we would be a blob of flesh. How we stand, walk, and move around depends on our bones. We must coordinate our bones and shift our weight around them to move.

- Protect our organs: The fact that our ribcage exists is no coincidence. It protects our organs from hard impacts, punctures, and other forms of injury. Our ribcage protects our lungs and heart. Our skull protects your brain.

- Production of blood cells: Strangely enough, our bones produce our red blood cells, platelets, and white blood cells. Platelets are responsible for blood clots, red blood cells deliver oxygens to various parts of our body, and white blood cells combat infections.

- Storing and releasing fat: Some bones also store and release fat when our body needs energy.

- Storing and releasing minerals: Bones keep necessary materials when too many are in our blood. Our bones can then release those back into the blood steam when our body needs them. One such mineral is calcium. Through a process called resorption, our bones can release calcium or store excess calcium based on its concentration in the bloodstream.

- Hormones control: Our bones also produce the precursors to various hormones, including those involved in insulin production, growth, and brain development. In addition, they release hormones that signal to the kidneys to regulate blood sugar and fat deposition.

- pH balance: Some research suggests that bones can also release or absorb alkaline salts, which help regulate the pH level in your blood.

Why is Bone Density Important?

Bone density is calculated by the amount of minerals present in a specific area of the bone. These minerals comprise 65% of the bone tissue, giving our bones their hardness and rigidity. As you might have guessed, bone density is an essential indicator of how likely bones are to break. It also identifies osteopenia and osteoporosis and assesses the effectiveness of treatment to minimize bone loss.

How Bones Change

When we're young, we often overlook the importance of strong bones. Our understanding of their role is limited to the fact that they support us and can break if we're not careful.

In reality, our bones are remarkable structures. They contain collagen fibers for flexibility and are fortified with calcium and phosphorus in a mineral called hydroxyapatite. They contribute 12-15% of our body weight and can withstand great stress.

It's not until later in life, usually after experiencing a fall resulting in a fracture or receiving a doctor's diagnosis of weakening bones, that we become more conscious of bone health.

It's crucial to comprehend that bones are living tissues that are constantly renewing. Every 5 to 10 years, our entire skeleton undergoes a renewal process. Although this process slows with age, we can assist in promoting bone revival.

Interestingly, we begin losing bone density from birth, but our bones replenish and surpass the loss, making them imperceptible. Around the age of 20, bones reach their peak density. However, deterioration occurs after approximately 50 years of age unless we lead a healthy lifestyle with adequate vitamin D, calcium, and exercise.

This decline in bone mass is more pronounced in women after menopause. At the same time, men experience a slower decline due to testosterone. Unfortunately, after the age of 65, everyone faces the same challenges. The risk of fracture doubles every five years from that point onward. With decreased bone density, spaces within the bones widen, and the outer walls become thinner. The danger lies in the fact that these changes are symptomless.

Surprisingly, about 43.3 million adults in the United States have osteopenia, which often goes unnoticed mainly because there is no pain associated with it. If left unchecked, osteopenia can progress to osteoporosis, affecting over 14 million people in the United States. Osteoporosis increases the likelihood of painful fractures, compromising mobility and quality of life. Spine fractures can lead to deformities and loss of height.

What Weakens Our Bones?

Other than age, there are a few more factors that contribute to bone density loss:

- Smoking
- Excessive alcohol consumption
- Sedentary lifestyle
- Certain health conditions (diabetes, chronic kidney disease, rheumatoid arthritis)
- Poor nutrition

- Low testosterone
- Decrease in estrogen (menopause)
- Certain medications
- Stress

The last point deserves more elaboration. Mental stress affects bone health due to the hormone cortisol. Cortisol, produced by cholesterol in the adrenal glands, can increase when exposed to daily stress, triggering the body's fight-or-flight response. While small amounts of cortisol are harmless, chronic stress leads to inflammation and elevated cortisol levels, compromising bone health.

Cortisol impacts bone density in three ways:

- It increases bone "resorption," the process where the body produces more bone-resorbing cells called osteoclasts, leading to decreased bone density.
- Cortisol blocks calcium from entering the bones, reducing the body's ability to reinforce them. This lack of material contributes to bone density loss over time.
- Elevated cortisol levels hinder the formation of new bone by impeding the action of bone-building cells known as osteoblasts, further compromising bone density.

In summary, increased stress gradually weakens bones.

What Causes Bone (Density) Growth?
Bones undergo a fascinating growth process that not everyone fully grasps. Babies have around 300 bones at birth, but this number decreases to 206 in adulthood. Baby bones are more petite and gradually fuse together, forming larger bones as they grow. Bone growth continues until the mid-20s, reaching maximum size.

The growth of bones involves several changes. Initially, a baby's bones mainly consist of flexible cartilage. As the baby grows, this cartilage expands, and through ossification, calcium replaces it.

During ossification, calcium and phosphate salts accumulate, enveloping the cartilage cells. These cells eventually die, creating small pockets in the bone that blood vessels penetrate, depositing specialized cells called osteoblasts.

Osteoblasts play a vital role in bone growth by collecting calcium within the pockets and producing collagen fibers that shape the bone's structure. Once the new bone is formed, the osteoblasts flatten and line the bone's surface, regulating calcium levels. Adequate calcium levels and other minerals are crucial for maintaining strong bones. Low calcium can decrease bone density and increase fracture risks.

Bone growth initiates at the ends of bones, particularly in the growth plates abundant with cartilage in babies. For long bones like those in the limbs, ossification begins at the center. It extends toward the ends, allowing for lengthening. By the mid-20s, the ossification process typically completes, and bones reach their maximum size.

Making Bones Stronger

Various types of exercise offer health benefits, but the most effective ones for building strong bones are weight-bearing and strength-training exercises. In addition, site-specific exercises can improve bone strength, with activities such as walking benefiting the legs and spine but not the wrist.

Postural stretching and strengthening can help older people prevent or decrease upper spine slumping, leading to spine fractures from activities such as bending over to tie shoes or cleaning. Maintaining good spine posture is crucial for all activities.

Weight-bearing exercises involve activities performed while standing that work bones and muscles against gravity. The more weight the bones bear, the harder they work, thus preventing further bone loss and promoting bone strength after young adulthood.

Some examples include walking, stair climbing, hiking, dancing, jumping rope, and hopscotch. In addition, sports like tennis, badminton, ping pong, and pickleball are good options.

While higher-impact activities like jogging and jumping rope offer more significant bone-strengthening benefits, frail individuals or those diagnosed with thinning bones should consult their doctors to determine the best physical activities for them.

Strength-Training Exercises

Resistance is added to movements during strength-training workouts to cause muscles to operate harder and become more powerful. Although these exercises primarily focus on increasing muscle mass, they also stress bones and have bone-building capacity.

Some typical strength-training exercises include weight machines, free weights, and exercises that use our body weight, such as push-ups. Elastic bands are also helpful in adding resistance to exercises to our routines. A general rule is to exercise each major muscle group at least twice weekly, with a full day of rest between workouts.

Other Forms of Exercise

While non-impact exercises such as yoga and tai chi are less effective at strengthening bones, they provide significant flexibility and balance benefits. Non-weight-bearing exercises like swimming, cycling, and chair exercises are also great for strengthening muscles and the heart and lungs, even though they don't increase bone density. Suppose you have a musculoskeletal health condition preventing you from weight-bearing activities. In that case, these are good alternatives to consider.

Beginning a Bone Health Fitness Program

To enhance bone health, a comprehensive exercise plan entails about 30 minutes of weight-bearing activity at least four days a week. Various types of weight-bearing exercises can provide us with diversification of activity and growth. Choose a few that you enjoy consistently and dive in.

You can complete the 30 minutes at once or split it into shorter intervals throughout the day. For example, brisk walking for 10 minutes, 2-3 times daily, is an excellent starting point.

If outdoor walking isn't possible, indoor alternatives like walking around your home, climbing stairs, or marching in place are practical weight-bearing exercises.

Include flexibility (stretching) and balance training to maximize the benefits of your exercise routine. Always begin and conclude with stretching to improve flexibility and agility, reduce injury risk, and promote relaxation.

When initiating a new exercise program, consider your risk of falling. Seek guidance from a physical therapist and consult your doctor to develop a safe exercise plan. For those with severe osteoporosis, be very cautious with upright weightlifting to avoid excessive spine compression (2-10 pounds may be safe). Avoid exercises involving twisting or bending the spine. Stationary bikes, rowing machines, and other weight machines may not be suitable for severe osteoporosis. Instead, consider safer alternatives like a chair and wall exercises.

Effects of Exercise on Bone Health

Physical activity alone does not significantly increase bone mass in adults after age 25. However, exercise can help prevent or slow bone loss and maintain muscle mass. Adequate nutrition, including calcium and vitamin D, is vital for preserving bone mass in both men and women.

Hormonal supplementation, like estrogens or androgens, may be necessary for middle-aged women and some men to maintain or improve bone mass. However, it's often not recommended for older adults with fragile bones. Instead, bone-preserving or bone-building medications are preferred.

For elderly adults, falls can result in fractures with long-term consequences, including permanent disability. The wrist, spine, and hip are common fracture sites. Fortunately, balance training and low-impact activities like Tai Chi can reduce falls by 47% and decrease the risk of hip fracture by around 25%! Additionally, men who engage in more vigorous physical activity tend to have a lower risk of hip fracture.

Breath Exercise

Breath, highly valued in ancient health practices, impacts overall health. In traditional Chinese medicine, eastern traditions like Ayurveda and Qi emphasize specific breathing exercises for optimal air energy intake. In the West, breathing is mainly recognized for oxygen supply, but its additional benefits are often overlooked.

Western science has started adopting Eastern insights and discovering the many advantages of deep nasal breathing. These include reducing blood pressure, enhancing tissue oxygenation, easing the heart's workload, improving sleep, and reducing negative emotional states like anger, confusion, fear, depression, or anxiety.

Ancient Eastern practices like qigong and yoga incorporate "bone marrow breathing" or "bone breathing," involving focused deep nasal breathing on different parts of the skeleton. Women practicing qigong experienced increased bone density, despite low-intensity exercise without bone loading. Yoga also positively impacts bone health, blood glucose regulation, mood enhancement, and heart function.

Deep breathing affects negative emotional states, which is relevant to bone health. Activation of lower lung lobes through deep breathing calms the parasympathetic fight-or-flight response, counteracting the detrimental effects of stress hormones like cortisol on bones. Deep nasal breathing is an easy, quick, and cost-effective method for improving overall health.

To promote bone health, begin practicing deep breathing using these simple steps:

- Find a comfortable seated position and tense and release your muscles, paying attention to the sensation of relaxation.
- Breathe slowly and naturally through your nostrils. Typically, our breathing is shallow, so start inhaling and exhaling more deeply without feeling like you're forcing it. Then, try inhaling through your nostrils only (count to 4), and exhale through your mouth (count to 8).
- Visualize your belly as if it contains your lungs and create a space to fill as you breathe in and out.
- Envision each breath as an energy source. Close your eyes and imagine a bright light powered by your breath, letting go of any serious or draining thoughts.
- Focus on your goals, such as relaxation or building energy. Use the provided chart for suggested inhalation, hold, and exhalation durations to achieve your goals.
- Keep up with your deep breathing for as long as it feels beneficial. If you start to worry about stopping, take a break. However, try to ignore these thoughts next time and continue for extended periods.

Get Enough Sleep

Did you know that getting 5 hours of sleep or less daily is associated with low bone mineral density and increased risks of osteoporosis? Research published in the Journal of Bone and Mineral Research involving 11,000 post-menopausal women found that insufficient sleep can negatively impact bone health. Women who slept 5 hours or fewer had remarkably lower bone mineral density in the hip, neck, spine, and whole body. On the other hand, those who slept 7 hours had higher bone mineral density, equivalent to slowing down aging by one year.

It's important to note that there was no noticeable difference in bone density among women who slept more than 7 hours. So, the sweet spot for sleep duration is 7-9 hours. During sleep, essential processes like bone remodeling occur, replacing old tissue with new bone tissue. Insufficient sleep limits the time available for this process, resulting in incomplete or improper bone remodeling.

While this may be concerning, the good news is that we have control over our sleep habits. Practicing good sleep hygiene, getting enough sleep, and adopting other healthy habits can positively impact our bone health. It's worth mentioning that poor sleep is also connected to other health problems like diabetes, high blood pressure, obesity, and cardiovascular issues. However, by taking charge of our sleep and overall well-being, we can exert control and influence over factors that affect our bone health.

Strength Training's Effects on Bones

We have already established that strength training will not just build but can help maintain muscle mass and strength. Having strong muscles can also contribute to having strong bones. And strong bones can minimize the risk of fractures.

Numerous studies show that strength training slows bone loss and may even increase bone mass. Stressing the bones through strength training activates bone-forming cells, combating factors contributing to bone loss.

Of course, the dose makes the poison as well. Too much stress on your bones can break them. That said, you can precisely control how much load your skeletal system gets as you learn how to properly move your muscles and weight. That load comes from the practice of pushing and pulling during strength training. What you get in the end are more robust, denser bones.

Strength training, in particular, has many benefits that aerobic exercises do not provide, such as:

- Weight management: Since exercises, in general, help us burn more calories, strength training enables us to manage our weight. Plus, it can increase our metabolism to help us burn even more calories.
- Improving the quality of life: Strength training can improve our quality of life and enhance our capacity to do everyday activities. It can also prevent injury by

strengthening our joints. Because strength training helps build muscles as well, it can contribute to better balance and lower our risk of falls.

- Managing chronic conditions: Strength training can improve chronic conditions like back pain, arthritis, obesity, heart disease, depression, and diabetes.
- Sharpening our mind: Some research suggests that regular strength training can help improve our learning and thinking skills.

Starting Out

If you have a chronic health condition or are over 40 and inactive, consult your doctor before starting a strength training or aerobic fitness program.

Before beginning any strength or balance training routine, warm up with about five to ten minutes of low-impact aerobic activity (like walking) to prevent muscle injury.

When working out, choose exercises that challenge you and cause fatigue after 12 to 15 repetitions. Increase weight or resistance when the exercise becomes too easy. Studies show that a single set of 12 to 15 repetitions with the right weight effectively builds muscle.

As mentioned, proper form is crucial and more important than the number of reps. Five reps with good form are better than 15 with poor form, which can lead to injury and ineffective muscle engagement.

On average, allow each muscle group one full day of rest between workouts for proper recovery. If you experience pain, listen to your body, lower the weight, or take a few days off.

To avoid injury, consider learning proper form and techniques from a local trainer or fitness specialist if you're new to strength training. Once you grasp the correct approach, you'll gain confidence and independence.

When to Expect Results

You don't have to expend hours each day lifting weights to reap the advantages of strength training. A few 30-minute strength training every week is enough for most people. You are not trying to look like Arnold Schwarzenegger here. You just want to be healthier.

For most healthy adults, the Department of Health and Human Services recommends the following exercise guidelines:

- Aerobic activity: 150 minutes of moderate-intensity or 75 high-intensity weekly activities is enough. You do not need to clock all those minutes in a single day. Instead, spread this exercise throughout the week. More training will provide more significant health benefits, but even small doses of physical activity are beneficial. Being active for a few minutes throughout the day goes a long way.
- Strength training: Exercise all major muscle groups at least twice per week. Seek to do a single set of each exercise, using a weight or resistance level heavy enough to fatigue your muscles after about 12 to 15 repetitions.

As you integrate strength training into your fitness routine, you will likely see improvements in your strength over time. With increased muscle mass, you'll probably be able to lift weights more efficiently and for extended periods. The most essential thing you need to do is to be consistent. Keep your routine to the best of your ability, even if there are no tangible results initially. <u>Eventually, you will be shocked by how many gains you can make by staying consistent</u>.

Positive Benefits of Stretching for Bones

The extent to which a joint can move in different directions, also known as its range of motion, is determined by various factors, including the internal mechanics of the joint and the structures that encompass it. Stretching exercises are beneficial in expanding this range of motion, and comprehending the function of these structures and how they can influence or impede a joint's flexibility is essential in understanding this process.

Joints serve as the connectors between bones. The movement that the bones can achieve is determined by the structure of each joint, such as whether it is a hinge, pivot, or ball-and-socket joint. Muscles surround joints and supply the energy necessary to move them. The degree of tension in the muscles surrounding a joint is crucial in determining how far the joint can move. Tissue scarring, habitual posture, involuntary muscle spasms, or deliberate muscle contractions can all affect muscle tension.

Tendons are connective tissues that join our muscles to our bones, making movement possible. Muscle energy is transmitted to the tendons as joints move, which pull on the bones. Ligaments are robust, fibrous bands of tissue that bind bone to bone or the cartilage at a joint. For example, the anterior cruciate ligament (ACL) is one of five ligaments that work together to regulate knee movement. Among other functions, the ACL helps prevent the knee joint from rotating too much.

When you stretch, you are targeting muscles and tendons rather than ligaments. Ligaments are not meant to be elastic. A ligament that is overly stretchy will not provide the stability and support required for safe movement.

Balancing Bones

Having stronger bones means having a solid foundation and frame for your body. They help reduce the risk of falling, improve posture, and support muscle muscles that help your balance and stability.

Here are seven ways how stronger bones contribute to balance:

- Stronger bones offer a more solid foundation for the body, making it easier to maintain balance as we move about.
- Stronger bones also help reduce the risk of falls, which is critical for seniors susceptible to bone fractures and other age-related dangers.
- Weight-bearing exercises can improve bone density and strength, improving overall balance.
- Stronger bones support the muscles.
- Stronger bones reduce the risk of osteoporosis, a condition that weakens the bones.
- Stronger bones can also help reduce the risk of fractures.

Effect of Drugs, Vitamins, and Foods on Bone Health

We will discuss this in more detail in the next chapter. Still, it is worth reviewing this to understand better how food and drugs can affect your bone health. So, first, let's talk about food.

- High-sodium foods: The saltier our food, the more calcium we lose. This loss is due to the salt triggering excessive calcium excretion through the kidneys.
- Sugary snacks: Although there is no direct link between sugar and bone health, the danger lies when we consume too much added sugar and do not get enough nutrient-rich foods.

- Soda: Drinking seven or more servings per week is related to decreased bone mineral density and increased fracture risk.
- Caffeine: Caffeine consumption contributes to low bone density. Combined with sugary foods, caffeine can have an even more pronounced effect on our bone health.
- Alcohol: Chronic and heavy alcohol consumption is linked to low bone mass, decreased bone formation, a higher risk of fractures, and more prolonged fracture healing.
- Legumes: Beans can prevent our body from absorbing calcium because they are rich in phytates. Beans can also benefit bone health by soaking them in water for a few hours to eliminate that substance.
- Inflammatory foods: Nightshade veggies can cause bone inflammation, leading to osteoporosis. Again, they should be avoided only partially since they contain nutrients promoting bone health. You only need to get enough calcium from them.
- Raw spinach and Swiss chard: They contain bone-healthy calcium and oxalates, which can prevent the calcium from being absorbed. You can still enjoy these greens if you pair them with another food source that contains calcium readily absorbed by the body.
- Red meat: Overeating animal protein can potentially leach calcium from your bones. You can still have red meat but keep your portions small.

What about medicine? Typically, your doctor will inform you about the potential side effects of your prescription, but if you haven't yet talked with your doctor about them, here is a short list:

- Corticosteroids: Prescribed for asthma and autoimmune disorders. These medications decrease bone formation.
- SSRIs: Selective serotonin inhibitors are frequently utilized to treat depression. Common SSRIs include Prozac and Lexapro. They, too, contribute to the loss of bone density.
- PPIs: Proton pump inhibitors are utilized to treat chronic acid reflux.
- Some diabetes medications: Actos, Invokana, etc.
- Anti-androgen medications: Used to treat prostate cancer.
- Some seizure medications: Tegretol, Dilantin, Depakote

- Loop diuretics: Water pills like Lasix and Bumex can also decrease the amount of calcium in your bones.
- Anti-estrogen medications: Used to treat certain types of breast cancer.
- Tramadol: Opioid pain medication that has many risks.
- Some transplant medications: Cyclosporine is one good example. It suppresses the immune system after an organ or bone marrow transplant.

Bone Evaluation

We'll discuss this more in the next chapter, but a bone density test is a non-invasive process used to measure the number of minerals, like calcium, in your bones. The most generally used test is the dual-energy X-ray absorptiometry (DXA), which can diagnose osteoporosis before a bone breaks, estimate the risk of future fractures, and monitor the effectiveness of treatments. The test is painless and only takes a few minutes, with very little radiation exposure. However, qualified staff is needed to perform and interpret the test correctly.

Women over 65 and men over 70, anyone who has broken a bone beyond age 50, and individuals with risk factors for osteoporosis should have a bone density test. Risk factors include family history, frequent falling, vitamin D deficiency, smoking, excessive alcohol intake, malabsorption, and certain medications.

Chapter Summary

- Our bones do much more than act as a foundation and a frame for our body. They also serve as a storage and blood cell production factory, among other functions.
- There is no pain in osteoporosis. It is silent, and there is no way of knowing if you have it until you run the tests.
- In the context of balance, bone density is the best measurement to determine the strength of one's bones. The denser the bones, the stronger they are.
- Our bones change throughout our lives. They are completely replaced every year, which is necessary to ensure that your bones remain strong. However, as we age, the body slowly loses its ability to "rebuild" our bones. Other than age, many other factors contribute to the loss of bone density.
- Luckily, there are many ways to strengthen our bones, including incorporating certain nutrients into our diets (calcium, vitamin D, etc.), exercising (balance and

weight-bearing training), getting enough sleep, stopping smoking and alcohol consumption, and even breathing.

• Considering that you will not know that your bones are weak until your legs give out underneath you. Getting tested is a good idea so you know where you are regarding your bone health.

4

THE ENEMY OF OSTEOPOROSIS

"How do I confront aging? With a wonder and a terror.
Yeah, I'll say that. Wonder and terror."
– Keanu Reeves

———

I f you've had any previous rudimentary knowledge of what osteoporosis is, you should basically know that it is an "enemy" of good health. But let's flip the phrase around for a second and say, "what is the enemy (or enemies) of osteoporosis"? By doing this, we should be able to more clearly define how to fight the condition by identifying effective weapons and tactics right out of the gate. But first, a quick story.

Sally Field's Story

Actress Sally Field has always portrayed strong women in her award-winning movie roles, reflecting her own self-image. Despite being known for her active lifestyle, including extreme yoga and outdoor activities, Field was diagnosed with osteoporosis just before turning 60. Osteoporosis occurs when bone-thinning occurs, leading to a higher risk of bone fractures.

As we age, our bone-building process slows, and bone loss intensifies. Women experience accelerated bone loss due to the significant drop in estrogen levels during menopause. Hormone replacement therapy (HRT) was a popular treatment option for hot flashes, mood swings, and bone protection until the Women's Health Initiative (WHI) discovered that the long-term use of blended estrogen and progestin boosted the risk of heart disease, stroke, and breast cancer. Field experienced a significant loss of bone density when she stopped taking HRT.

Field took a proactive stance and decided to treat her osteoporosis with a new once-monthly medication called Boniva, which slows bone loss and allows natural bone production. Field has also become an advocate for osteoporosis awareness, teaming up with the makers of Boniva to spearhead an awareness campaign. Despite concerns about side effects, Field believes the benefits of taking charge of her osteoporosis far outweigh any risks.

Why do I mention this celebrity account here? Well, it's to show you two sides to the story and to assist you along the path of making informed decisions for your bone health.

You see, the drug Boniva (and its competitors) have some controversy around them. In an article written by the online journal called Save Our Bones, the author Vivian Goldschmidt "rewrites" and parodies the advertisement that Fields did for Bonita.

Without going into too much detail, Goldschmidt counters the advantages of the drug by describing how it's detrimental to bones and then provides alternative natural solutions for combating osteoporosis that are safer and more effective. It's an interesting assertion, but who is right?

The answer to that would probably require its own book or lengthy article to look at all the data and the pros and cons of each. If you have osteoporosis or osteopenia (the precursor), I encourage you to dig into the data (at least online) to discover if a pharmaceutical or natural approach is better for you.

What is Osteoporosis?

Before we jump into Osteoporosis' enemies, let's define it. Osteoporosis is characterized by decreased bone mass, resulting in bones that appear normal from the outside but become porous inside due to the loss of calcium and phosphate as we age.

This loss can cause your bone to be more brittle and break more easily, even during simple activities such as standing, walking, or bathing. Often, the disease goes unnoticed until a fracture occurs.

The basic prevention for treating osteoporosis is consuming a balanced diet rich in calcium, phosphorous, and vitamin D and engaging in regular exercise (especially strength training) that is approved by a healthcare professional. As mentioned, medications can also be used as part of a treatment plan and should be researched and discussed thoroughly with a healthcare provider.

In addition to not consuming enough high-calcium foods and vitamin D, other factors that contribute to bone loss include:

- Decreased estrogen and testosterone levels.
- Prolonged bed rest.
- Certain medical conditions cause inflammation in the body.
- Taking certain medications.

Risk factors also include the absence of menstrual periods, a family history of osteoporosis, excessive alcohol consumption, low body weight, smoking, eating disorders, and being part of certain ethnic groups with a higher prevalence of low bone mass.

Who is At Risk?

Contrary to popular belief, osteoporosis is not limited to senior Caucasian women. It can impact people of all ages and ethnicities, including men. Age is a significant factor, with bone density peaking around 30 and decreasing afterward. Engaging in weight-bearing exercises and consuming sufficient calcium and vitamin D can help maintain our bone strength as we age.

Gender also plays a crucial role, with women over 50 at the highest risk, although men can still develop osteoporosis. Family history, body weight, and bone structure are additional factors. Ethnicity also plays a role, with Caucasian and Asian women having a higher probability of developing osteoporosis.

Certain diseases, medications like long-term steroid use, smoking, and heavy alcohol consumption increase the risk. Avoiding these factors is recommended for optimal bone health.

Signs and Symptoms

Osteoporosis is a condition that often presents no noticeable symptoms. Sometimes, individuals only become aware of it after experiencing a minor injury or fall resulting in a bone fracture. Waiting for such an accident to occur before getting tested for osteoporosis is never a good idea.

The U.S. Preventive Services Task Force strongly recommends that women over 65 undergo screening for osteoporosis, and those younger than 65 who are at higher risk should also consider getting tested. In addition, while men generally lose bone density slower than women, they should still be aware of the possibility of developing osteoporosis, particularly older men prone to bone fractures or at risk for osteoporosis.

Healthcare providers can perform a bone density scan to determine the strength of one's bones by comparing it to that of an average healthy young adult. This test result, known as a T-score, can indicate whether a person has osteoporosis or osteopenia, a low bone density less severe than osteoporosis. Doctors may also employ other screening tools such as questionnaires, physical exams, and ultrasounds to predict the likelihood of having low bone density or sustaining a bone fracture.

Primary and Secondary Osteoporosis

Physicians classify osteoporosis into two categories: primary and secondary.

Primary osteoporosis occurs because of aging. In women, the hormones estrogen and progesterone decrease following menopause. These hormones are crucial for maintaining healthy bones, and reduced levels make it difficult for the body to generate new, strong bone tissue.

Secondary osteoporosis, on the other hand, arises due to an underlying medical condition or the use of specific medications that hinder the body's capacity to produce new bone tissue.

The Enemies: Commitment, Prevention, Treatment

Commitment

Let's start by first singling out one of the worst enemies. You could say it is the "arch enemy" of osteoporosis and any other health condition for that matter. And that is "commitment." Without committing to searching out solutions for our health problems, there truly can be no answers, right? Without being proactive, nothing is going to get better. So as long as we commit (and you already have by reading this book), we can be confident that we're already on the right path. So don't stop. Keep on peeling the onion back for answers. Stay committed.

Prevention

To prevent osteoporosis on the most basic level, it's crucial to maintain a healthy diet, exercise regularly, and avoid smoking. Both men and women should follow these recommendations.

Exercise: Exercise can improve bone mass in premenopausal women and help maintain bone density in menopausal women, as well as strengthen muscles, improve balance, and reduce the risk of falls. Experts recommend exercising for at least 30 minutes three times a week, minimum. Weight-bearing, aka strength training exercises, should be a part of those routines.

Diet: A healthy diet rich in protein, calories, calcium, and vitamin D is crucial for maintaining proper bone formation and density.

Calcium intake: Women and men should consume at least 1000 mg of calcium daily, including calcium from supplements. Postmenopausal women should consume 1200 mg per day. However, taking more than 2000 mg per day can cause side effects. Sources of calcium include milk, dairy products, and green vegetables. Your healthcare provider may suggest supplements if you don't consume enough calcium.

Vitamin D intake: Men over 70 years and postmenopausal women should consume 800 international units of vitamin D per day. Although the optimal intake for premenopausal women or younger men with osteoporosis has yet to be verified, 600 international units daily are generally suggested.

Minimize alcohol: Drinking more than two drinks a day can increase the fracture risk.

No smoking: Smoking can speed up bone loss, so quitting is strongly recommended.

Avoiding falls: Taking measures to prevent falls can reduce the likelihood of fractures in older adults, such as removing tripping hazards, providing adequate lighting, and avoiding walking on slippery surfaces.

Avoid medications that increase risk: Certain medications, such as glucocorticoid and heparin, can increase bone loss. You can minimize your risk of osteoporosis by stopping or changing these medications.

Treatments

There are various medications and treatments available to treat osteoporosis. One class of medications used to treat osteoporosis is hormone and hormone-related therapy. This process includes estrogen, testosterone, and the selective estrogen receptor modulator raloxifene (Evista).

Estrogen therapy is typically used in women who need to manage menopause symptoms or in younger women but may come with certain risks. Testosterone may be prescribed for men with low levels of this hormone to increase bone density. Raloxifene acts similarly to estrogen with the bones and may also minimize the risk of breast cancer in some women. Calcitonin-salmon (Fortical and Miacalcin) is a synthetic hormone that can reduce the risk of spine fractures but is not recommended as a first-choice treatment due to potential side effects.

Bisphosphonates are another class of medications used to treat osteoporosis. These drugs are antiresorptive and prevent the body from reabsorbing bone tissue. Several formulations are available, including alendronate, ibandronate, risedronate, and zoledronic acid. Bisphosphonates may be taken for three to five years, providing benefits after stopping. Still, they can also come with potential side effects such as flu-like symptoms, heartburn, and impaired kidney function.

Biologics like denosumab (Prolia) may be an option when other treatments fail. This medication is given as an injection every six months. Still, it can also have serious side effects, such as bone problems in the thigh or jaw and severe infections.

Anabolic agents are medications that build bone in people with osteoporosis. For example, Romososumab-aqqg (Evenity) is approved for postmenopausal women at high risk of fracture and enables new bone formation while decreasing breakdown. Teriparatide (Forteo) and Abaloparatide (Tymlos) are injectable drugs that mimic parathyroid hormones and are given daily for two years.

Other Medicinal Solutions

You may have questions regarding therapy. For example, are you taking the most suitable medication? What is the duration of treatment? Why did your doctor prescribe a weekly pill while your friend takes a monthly pill? Your healthcare provider can certainly work with you to answer these questions and determine the most suitable option, but it's important to know what solutions are available so you can ask the best questions.

The first-line medications include bisphosphonates like alendronate (Fosamax), taken weekly, and risedronate (Actonel), taken weekly or monthly. Ibandronate (Boniva) is taken monthly or quarterly via intravenous infusion, while zoledronic acid (Reclast) is given once a year via IV infusion.

Denosumab (Prolia, Xgeva) is an alternative for those who can't take bisphosphonates. It involves injections every six months. Treatment duration may be long-term, and stopping denosumab carries a risk of spinal fractures, so consistency is essential.

Bisphosphonate pills can cause stomach upset and heartburn. To minimize side effects, avoid lying down or bending over for 30 to 60 minutes after taking them. Taking the pills with water on an empty stomach and waiting before eating or drinking can also help.

Rare complications include atypical femoral fractures and osteonecrosis of the jaw, which is more typical in cancer patients taking higher bisphosphonate doses.

Natural Solutions

We'll do a deeper dive into nutrition in Chapter 6, but here is a quick list of foods and their associated nutrients that can help to improve bone health:

- Dairy products are rich in calcium. Some dairy products are also fortified with vitamin D.
- Canned sardines and salmon (with bones) are excellent sources of calcium, while fatty fish like salmon, mackerel, tuna, and sardines are rich in vitamin D.

- Leafy greens like turnip greens, kale, okra, Chinese cabbage, dandelion greens, etc., are high in calcium and vitamin K.

- Magnesium-rich foods include spinach, beet greens, okra, tomato derivatives, artichokes, plantains, potatoes, sweet potatoes, greens, prunes, and raisins.

- Potassium-rich foods include tomato products, prunes, raisins, potatoes, spinach, sweet potatoes, papaya, oranges, orange juice, bananas, and plantains.

- Vitamin C-rich foods include red peppers, green peppers, oranges, grapefruits, broccoli, strawberries, brussels sprouts, papaya, and pineapples.

- Foods high in vitamin K include dark leafy greens such as kale, collard greens, spinach, mustard greens, turnip greens, and Brussels sprouts.

- Fortified foods such as juices, breakfast foods, soy milk, rice milk, cereals, snacks, and bread may also contain calcium and vitamin D.

Other Foods That May Boost Bone Health

Recent research suggests that blueberries, olive oil, fish oil, soybeans, and other foods high in omega-3s, may also be bone-boosting. One study has also surprisingly revealed that moderate consumption of certain alcoholic and non-alcoholic beverages, such as wine, beer, and tea, may benefit bone health. Specifically, slowing bone turnover rate. But more investigation is needed, however, to understand this relationship better. There is evidence that moderate to heavy drinking can increase the risk of osteoporosis as well as other health issues, so it's better to err on the side of caution here and dial back any heavy drinking.

Tips for Eating for Good Bone Health

It's significant to note that some foods may not be ideal for bone health. Here is a quick rundown:

- Beans contain calcium, magnesium, and fiber. Still, they are also high in phytates, which interfere with the body's ability to absorb calcium. Soak beans in water for 2-3 hours before cooking them in fresh water to reduce phytate levels.

- While getting enough protein for overall health is essential, consuming too much protein from meat and other high-protein foods can cause the body to lose calcium. Try to obtain enough calcium from sources like dairy products containing protein.

- Consuming many salty foods can lead to bone loss because salt causes the body to lose calcium. Avoid processed and canned foods and foods with high salt content.

Look for the daily value of sodium on the nutrition facts label and aim for no more than 2,300mg of sodium per day.

- Foods with oxalates, such as spinach, rhubarb, beet greens, and certain beans, contain other nutrients but should not be counted as sources of calcium since oxalates interfere with calcium absorption.
- Wheat bran includes high levels of phytates that prevent the absorption of calcium in other foods consumed at the same time. When consumed together, 100% wheat bran cereal may reduce calcium absorption in milk.
- Alcohol can lead to bone loss, so limit your consumption.
- Consuming caffeine from coffee, tea, and soft drinks in moderation is recommended since caffeine can interfere with calcium absorption and contribute to bone loss. Drinking more than three cups of coffee every day can interfere with calcium absorption and cause bone loss.

Bone Assessment

While it's best to prevent bone loss and osteoporosis from occurring in the first place, it's possible to avoid further loss of bone mass and strength if we are diagnosed. Studies are inconclusive that exercise programs may significantly improve bone mineral density in osteoporosis patients. However, studies have shown that osteoporosis treatments and exercise can improve other determinants of bone strength, such as bone quality and turnover, which can significantly help to reduce fracture risk.

Taking the proper steps can improve your bone strength and overall health. If you feel at risk for osteoporosis or fractures, don't hesitate to speak to your doctor about getting bone density tested and developing a plan to improve your bone health.

Bone Density Testing

A Bone Density Test, also known as a DEXA or DXA scan, is a low-radiation X-ray that measures bone mineral density to identify the risk of osteoporosis. The procedure is non-invasive, quick, and usually requires no preparation. The test results are reported in two categories: T-score and Z-score.

The T-score compares a patient's bone mineral density with a healthy young adult of the identical gender. A T-score of -1 or above is considered normal. At the same time, a score between -1 and -2.5 indicates osteopenia or early stages of bone loss. A score of -2.5 or lower indicates established osteoporosis.

The Z-score, on the other hand, compares a patient's bone density with that of people of the same age, gender, and ethnicity. This score is used for children, premenopausal women, and men under 50. Suppose a patient's Z-score is lower or higher than the average. In that case, healthcare professionals may recommend further monitoring and testing to identify any underlying medical conditions or medication use that may contribute to further bone density decline.

Overall, bone density testing is an essential diagnostic tool that helps doctors evaluate a patient's bone health and identify the risk of osteoporosis. It can also guide treatment decisions and prevent fractures, breaks, and sprains.

Why and Who

Bone density testing is crucial for identifying osteoporosis early and starting treatment promptly. In addition, testing and treatments can prevent patients from experiencing broken bones and other complications.

There are several risk factors to consider when determining who should undergo bone density testing. The International Society of Bone Densitometry recommends testing for women aged 65 and older, post-menopausal women younger than 65 with certain risk factors such as low body weight, prior fractures, or high-risk medication use, men aged 70 and older, and adults with conditions or on medications associated with low bone mass or bone loss.

In summary, bone density testing is a valuable tool for assessing bone health and identifying the risk of osteoporosis. In addition, it can guide treatment decisions and help prevent complications such as fractures, breaks, and sprains.

When?

The timing for getting a bone density test depends on individual risk factors and health history. For example, your doctor may recommend a test after experiencing a fracture, reaching a certain age, or having decreased hormone levels. While osteoporosis screening is commonly recommended for women 65 and older, younger women and men may also need to be tested based on their risk factors.

To prepare for a DXA test, there is usually no need for any specific measures. However, if you take calcium supplements, your doctor may advise you to discontinue them 24 hours before the test.

Bear Bones: A Solution in Bears?

Human bones begin to weaken after just a few days of bed rest. If this period of inactivity goes beyond several weeks, it could lead to osteoporosis and broken bones. In contrast, bears hibernate for several months, but when they wake up in spring, their bones remain as strong as before their hibernation. This presents an interesting conundrum that is being researched.

Associate professor of biomedical engineering at Michigan Tech, Seth Donahue, has studied bear physiology to unravel the mechanism that protects bears from osteoporosis.

Bear bones also release minerals just like ours. But interestingly, bears reabsorb it and put it back in their bones. Donahue hypothesizes that bears have such healthy bones due to the actions of the parathyroid hormone, which may be more efficient in bears than in humans when it comes to transporting minerals back into the bones.

To test this hypothesis, Donahue and his team made their supply of bear parathyroid hormone by cloning the gene responsible for producing the hormone from samples of American black bear blood provided by another research study, using E. coli bacteria for manufacturing it.

With a grant from the National Institutes of Health, Donahue and his team have conducted two experiments using the bear hormone with hopes of developing a new and more effective treatment for human osteoporosis.

In the first experiment, they grew human bone-making cells in the lab, which they will treat with either human or bear parathyroid hormone to determine the distinctions between the two groups. In preliminary studies, the bear parathyroid hormone prevented cell death better than the human parathyroid hormone and robustly affected human bone formation signaling pathways.

Donahue also chairs the scientific advisory board for Aursos. This small biotech company applied to the Food and Drug Administration to use the recombinant bear parathyroid hormone to treat osteoporosis. If the studies go well, the hormone could potentially be used in humans, but it would take years to develop.

Chapter Summary

- Osteoporosis is distinguished by a reduction in bone mass, making you more susceptible to fractures even during routine activities like walking, standing, or bathing.

- Osteoporosis is not just limited to older adults, as many other factors affect bone density.

- Primary osteoporosis occurs because of aging, whereas secondary osteoporosis arises due to a medical condition or the use of certain medications.

- Prevention is the best medicine. Changing one's diet goes a long way in maintaining bone density. Consider incorporating more calcium and vitamin D into your diet.

- Exercise can also improve bone mass and muscle strength, improving overall agility and balance.

- Your doctor may also recommend you take some medications to improve your bone health but discuss possible side effects and interactions with other existing medications.

- Limiting or eliminating alcohol, caffeine, and smoking will go a long way for your bone and overall health.

- Although numerous studies have been done to discover a more effective treatment for osteoporosis (one involving bears!), it will still take a long time before any practical solutions can be found. Even then, one should rely on something other than medicine to fix every health problem. Again, prevention is better than curing something; nothing beats a healthy lifestyle.

5

MORE THAN MERE POSTURING

"I want to get old gracefully. I want to have good posture;
I want to be healthy and be an example to my children."
– Sting.

————

Just like parts of our cars, every piece of our bodies will weaken due to wear and tear. Assuming we have good posture, every detail will wear down at a very slow but even pace, which is what we want. However, lousy posture puts stress on certain parts of our bodies, weakening specific muscles, overworking others, compressing our organs, and causing our bodies to be unbalanced.

Over time, these overworked and weakened parts cause pain, meaning they are not working efficiently. In this compromised position, your body will need to use extra energy to make sure you stay upright.

Posture Defined

Simply put, posture refers to the positions of different joints of our bodies at a given moment. It is how we hold our bodies. Standing up straight is one component, but there is more to posture than that. The position of each joint directly affects the function of other joints. There are two types of postures:

- Dynamic: How we hold ourselves when moving, such as walking, running, etc.

- Static: How we hold ourselves when we are stationary such as sleeping, sitting, or standing.

For both static and dynamic postures, our spine plays a significant role. Personal trainers may use a broomstick to illustrate how you should have a neutral spine (not flexing in any way) during specific exercises, but that is only there for just that – illustration. In reality, our spine has three natural curves - one at the lower back, one at the mid back, and one at the neck.

Why is posture important? Simply put, our bodies have an intricate system for balance as we move about. Our muscles, joints, bones, tendons, ligaments, etc., work together to ensure that we can stand and walk upright.

How Posture Affects Us

Bad postures can do a lot more damage than we may realize. Here are some examples of what can happen as a result:

Misalignment of Bones

Maintaining good posture, also known as the neutral position, is crucial to align our bones precisely, balancing our body, and facilitating healthy movement. With each activity, mainly walking or running, our bones experience significant shock and stress.

Proper body alignment through good posture helps distribute pressure among multiple structures, preventing injuries by ensuring that no bone, muscle, or joint takes on more stress than it can handle.

When our posture deviates from the neutral position, our body compensates by exerting more pressure on one structure, creating an imbalance that can cause injuries and limit our ability to stay active.

Back and Neck Pain

The natural curves of our spine distribute our weight, add flexibility, and absorb the shock caused by movement. If our vertebrae sit directly on top of each other in a straight line, our spine would be vulnerable to injuries and degeneration from excessive stress.

Poor posture resulting from prolonged sitting, standing, bending, or slouching flattens our spinal curves, making us susceptible to disc damage, slipped vertebrae, pinched nerves, and other problems that cause chronic back and neck pain.

Additionally, looking down (or sideways in bed) at our smartphone or other electronic devices for extended periods can cause neck pain and stiffness due to the 50-pound stress on our neck caused by the head's bending.

Joint Damage

Repeated movements, weight-bearing, and pressure transfer between bones put significant pressure on our joints. In addition, poor posture throws our body's balance, forcing your joints to manage more stress and shock than they can handle. This extra wear and tear accelerates degenerative changes and leads to joint injuries and arthritis.

Torn Soft Tissues

Bad posture also affects the proper functioning of muscles, ligaments, and tendons that support our musculoskeletal system. These supporting soft tissues are designed to share stress, with one muscle absorbing some and passing the rest on to other tissues.

However, changes in our posture disrupt this system, and some muscles bear more stress than others, causing injuries ranging from muscle fatigue and cramps to stress fractures and painful tears.

Breathing Difficulties

Poor posture not only affects our musculoskeletal system but also causes breathing difficulties. For example, when our posture bends the spine, it contracts our rib cage, reducing the space around our lungs, affecting our diaphragm, and making it hard to take a deep breath.

Balance Issues

Coordination between bones, joints, muscles, and your sensory system is essential for maintaining balance during movements such as twisting, turning, bending, or sudden responses like catching a falling object. Unfortunately, chronic poor posture throws off this system, causing balance problems that make moving challenging.

Why We Need Good Posture

As we age, our spines undergo changes such as thinning and breakdown of the vertebrae and discs, as well as loss of thickness and elasticity in cartilage and connective tissues. However, maintaining proper posture throughout our lives can help minimize height loss and keep the bones in our spine healthy and strong. For seniors, proper posture is even more crucial, as it offers numerous benefits, including:

- Reduced risk of falls, which are the leading causes of injury among seniors.
- Prevention of conditions such as osteoporosis and osteoarthritis, which can result from overworked muscles and ligaments due to poor posture.
- Reduced risk of hypertension, stroke, heart attack, and other health problems associated with poor blood flow.
- Improved mood and reduced feelings of depression due to better circulation and oxygenation of the body.
- Enhanced cognitive functioning and better memory recall through improved communication between neurotransmitters and the brain.
- Improved digestion and blood flow by sitting up straight while eating, preventing organ compression.
- More successful execution of daily tasks from computer work to playing the piano to exercise.

We need to be mindful of maintaining proper posture to experience these benefits, which can involve adjustments to sitting and standing positions and regular exercise to strengthen the muscles supporting the spine.

Posture Solutions

Just like many things in life, we do not have to sit there and accept our fate. There are many things we can do to improve our posture.

Breathing

How we breathe significantly impacts our body, regulating essential functions such as heart rate and blood pressure and promoting proper body mechanics that reduce stress as we move.

Deep breathing, also called belly breathing, involves slowly inhaling deeply through the nose, causing the lungs to fill with air as the belly expands. This type of breathing has numerous health benefits, including stress reduction and lower blood pressure.

However, many people have developed a habit of shallow breathing due to the fast pace of life and sedentary work environments. This weakens the respiratory muscles over time and creates tension in the upper body, negatively affecting posture and overall health.

If you are a shallow breather, incorporating regular physical activity and respiratory muscle training can help alleviate these symptoms and enhance your quality of life.

How does breathing work?

The respiratory muscles surrounding our lungs contract and expand to inhale and exhale air. The diaphragm, a dome-shaped muscle in the lower ribs at the base of the chest, is the primary muscle used during inhalation. When the diaphragm contracts, it creates room in the chest cavity, allowing the lungs to inflate.

The intercostal muscles, located between the ribs, aid the diaphragm by raising the rib cage and allowing more air to enter the lungs. Other muscles near the neck and collarbone, such as the sternocleidomastoid, serratus anterior, pectoralis minor, and scalene, can assist the intercostals if breathing becomes difficult. These muscles increase the speed and amount of movement the ribs can achieve.

How Posture and Breathing Affect Movement

How we breathe and hold our posture can significantly influence our movements. For example, breathing from our chest area relies on secondary muscles near our neck and collarbone rather than our diaphragm, causing poor posture that can hinder multiple muscles in our upper body from functioning correctly.

As we remain seated for extended periods, our body's ability to resist gravity and maintain a sturdy, stable core diminishes. In addition, tight accessory muscles surrounding our chest can force our shoulders forward, causing a hunched posture and weakened back, as they restrict the activity of muscles essential for an upright stance, such as the latissimus dorsi, middle trapezius, rhomboids, and quadratus lumborum muscle.

Additionally, tight accessory muscles can lead to shoulder instability and impingement syndromes, as they limit the movement of tendons and muscles responsible for moving your shoulder blades, including the serratus anterior, biceps tendon, posterior deltoid, supraspinatus, and infraspinatus.

Studies indicate that people with ongoing mild-to-moderate neck pain or stiff neck muscles face difficulties in utilizing their lungs and respiratory system to their fullest potential, resulting in further limitations in their movement.

Promoting Correct Breathing Techniques

Slow, steady breathing patterns can enhance core stability, boost endurance during high-intensity workouts, and reduce the risk of muscle fatigue and injury. Therefore, your aim should be to take balanced, equal breaths.

To practice balanced breathing, try taking a deep inhale, counting to four, and then exhaling deeply for the exact count.

If you're unsure whether you're breathing shallowly, place your palm on your abdomen beneath your rib cage, exhale, and then take a deep breath. Observe the movement of your hand. If your hand moves when your stomach expands, you're breathing correctly.

Suppose your hand moves only slightly and your shoulders elevate. In that case, you may need to practice breathing exercises to strengthen your muscles and support proper breathing patterns.

Deep breathing exercises and general fitness training can strengthen your respiratory muscles. Techniques like roll breathing can also help you achieve full use of your lungs while controlling your breathing rhythm.

Other Tips for Improving Posture and Balance

Here are five strategies to help improve your posture and balance by straightening your spine:

- Practice Yoga or Tai Chi: These practices emphasize strength, flexibility, and body awareness. Studies show that practicing yoga or Tai Chi can improve scores on tests of postural control, balance, flexibility, and muscle strength in people with Parkinson's disease.

- Consult a Physical Therapist: Physical therapists are experts in improving physical function and can help address individual posture and balance challenges. They can assess your limitations and design a customized program for you, incorporating exercises that strengthen muscles in the back, shoulders, and other areas that support good posture. Physical therapists can also teach activities to improve postural problems associated with Parkinson's disease.

- Self-check your posture: Use a mirror several times a day to view your posture from the front and sides to ensure that you stand up straight and maintain good posture.

- Try exergames: Computer-based exercise games like Nintendo Switch's Ring Fit Adventure can be an unconventional yet fun and effective way to improve balance. Studies have shown that such games can significantly improve balance compared to traditional balance training.

- Increase bone health: Osteoporosis can cause spinal vertebrae to compress, leading to poor posture and pain. To prevent osteoporosis, engage in weight-bearing exercise, consume a diet high in calcium, and ensure adequate vitamin D intake. In addition, consult your doctor to assess your risk of osteoporosis and consider bone density scans or medications to improve bone health.

Aging's Effect on Flexibility

As we grow older, our bodies naturally become less flexible. This is due to various factors such as reduced water content in tissues and the spine, stiffening of joints, and decreased elasticity in muscle tendons and surrounding tissue. Unfortunately, this loss of flexibility can impact our ability to enjoy activities we once loved, affecting our daily lives. Many people further limit their physical activities because they believe they are inflexible, which exacerbates the situation.

The principle of "Use It or Lose It" governs our body's functioning. Failing to exercise our muscles results in strength loss and a decline in flexibility, especially if we don't maintain the full range of motion in our muscles. However, there is good news: we can delay or even reverse some of these changes in our bodies. While it may not be possible to prevent all flexibility loss, we can prevent loss of function caused by reduced flexibility.

As we age, our capacity to move our joints to their fullest extent decreases. The average person experiences a decline of 25%-30% in overall flexibility by the time they reach 70 years of age, with some joints more affected than others. For instance, a study found that shoulder flexion decreased by 15% between individuals aged 20-30 and those aged 70. In comparison, another study noted a 30% reduction in hamstring flexibility in the same age groups.

Several factors contribute to this decline, including stiffness of tendons and ligaments, decreased elastin content, wear and tear of cartilage, ligaments, and tendons, reduced synovial fluid, and dysfunction of muscles surrounding the joint.

However, engaging in physical activity can significantly slow down this decline in flexibility. Research has shown that physically active individuals have a much greater range of motion, even as they age.

Flexibility serves as a functional marker of aging, reflecting the function of specific organs or systems in the body and showing a link with age. Moreover, flexibility markers can improve with targeted interventions. Consequently, it is important to include flexibility measurements in comprehensive evaluations of health and aging. For example, incorporating appropriate stretching exercises can slow down the decline in shoulder joint range of motion associated with age, leading to better overall health.

Benefits of Stretching for Posture

There are many benefits of stretching, and they all apply to people of all ages. It does not matter whether you work in construction, an office worker, an athlete, etc., simple stretching offers something to everybody.

Reduces Lower Back Pain and Arthritis

Stretching can alleviate low back pain and arthritis, which are common among older adults. These conditions are typically caused by osteoarthritis and spinal stenosis, resulting in cartilage degeneration between facet joints and narrowing of the bone channel occupied by spinal nerves or cords.

While aging-related osteoarthritis and spinal stenosis are unavoidable, stretching exercises can help manage pain. Regular stretching can improve flexibility, range of motion, and elasticity, relieving stiffness. Although it may be painful and challenging to move these joints, warming up stiff muscles with a heat pack before stretching and cooling down muscles with an ice pack after exercise can reduce pain and swelling. Using stretching equipment or seeking assistance from another individual for assisted stretching may also be helpful.

Reduces Risk of Falling

Research has demonstrated that regular stretching is crucial for enhancing balance and stability, reducing the risk of falls. Enhancing flexibility in the hamstrings, quadriceps, and lower back is essential to prevent falls and improve hip joint mobility. In addition, these stretching exercises can help to prevent falls by promoting excellent stability and balance in the body.

Improve Poor Posture

As we age, the water content in connective tissue, such as ligaments and tendons, decreases, reducing elasticity and flexibility. The tightening of ligaments and tendons in the chest and shoulders, combined with years of sitting in a hunched position at a desk, can gradually result in poor posture. Inadequate posture is characterized by a forward head position, rounded shoulders and upper back, and hips pressing forward, compressing the natural S-curve of the spine and causing pain in the lower back and between the shoulder blades.

Improving flexibility can be accomplished through a consistent stretching regimen. This will help to loosen tight ligaments, tendons, and muscles, enhancing your range of motion. Furthermore, incorporating senior strength training exercises into your routine, along with stretching, will help to balance out weaker muscles, correcting poor posture and promoting flexibility.

Stretching Improves Blood Flow and Energy Levels

Dynamic stretching is a type of low-intensity stretching that employs movement to elongate our muscles, as opposed to static stretching, which involves stretching while our body is motionless. Dynamic stretches lengthen our muscles and promote circulation and nutrient flow throughout the body, increasing energy levels. This is particularly important for older adults, as increased energy can help maintain independence, foster social engagement, and support healthy aging.

Chapter Summary

- Posture refers to the positions of different joints of your body at a given moment. In other words, it is how you hold up your body.

- Posture is a lot more than just sitting up straight, however. Proper posture does not overload specific muscles or joints. Poor posture throws off your body's balance, which your body tries to compensate for, leading to more wear and tear on your bones, muscles, and organs, which requires more energy.

- Other than being conscious about how you move about, proper breathing, practicing Tai Chi or yoga, stretching, and eating the right food will go a long way in promoting good posture.

- Flexibility and stretching are important components of maintaining good posture and should be included in our daily routines.

6

NUTRITION FOR BALANCE AND BONES

*"It's all about nutrition. You can train, train, train all you want
but I always say you can't out-train a bad diet."*
– Joe Wicks

———

Before we dive into this chapter, please understand that this is purely a "launching point" into basic nutrition for balance and bones. This book is technically not a "nutrition book" but merely a guide to starting you on a path of nutritional discovery. With that disclaimer, let's start peeling back this figurative nutritional onion just a bit.

Why Good Nutrition is Crucial

First of all, maintaining good bone health and preventing osteoporosis all start with the proverbial "well-balanced diet." As it relates to this chapter, "well-balanced" means an adequate intake of nutrients essential for bone formation. These include calcium, protein, magnesium, phosphorus, vitamin D, and potassium. Furthermore, other vitamins and minerals, including manganese, copper, boron, iron, zinc, vitamin A, vitamin K, vitamin C, and the B vitamins, play a vital role in normal bone metabolism and should be included in the diet.

Supplements for nutrients such as calcium and vitamin D (and others) may be essential for individuals who cannot meet the recommended nutrient levels through diet alone.

Phytoestrogens (compounds that occur naturally in plants) are also potential power sources for bone health. While data points to their effectiveness in helping with things like hot flashes, acne, menstrual irregularities, and preventing bone loss, further research is still needed to determine the specific effects of phytoestrogens.

While we should increase our consumption of good foods high in the above nutrients, vitamins, and minerals, we should also reduce our intake of things like caffeine, phytic and oxalic acids (which can prevent calcium from being absorbed), sugar, ethanol (yes, you heard that right), and other additives and dietary components that can negatively impact bone health.

It is also necessary to know that certain medications can interfere with nutrient absorption and negatively affect bone health. As always, please check with your doctor about these potential effects when being prescribed medications.

In addition to increasing the "good stuff" and decreasing the "bad stuff," adopting a healthy lifestyle by incorporating regular physical activity can help maintain bone mass and decrease the risk of bone loss. Creating a routine of consistent, safe exercise in your lifestyle is the most effective approach for empowering the nutrients that we put into our bodies. While nothing in life is guaranteed, this one-two punch is our best chance at not falling and getting seriously hurt.

Story of Bobby Clay

To illustrate how vital nutrition is for our bones and overall health, let us quickly look at the elite British athlete Bobby Clay. Clay, an aspiring young runner, was in the middle of chasing her dreams for the 2016 Olympic team. Out of nowhere, she suffered a devastating setback when diagnosed with osteoporosis at the age of 18. The cause? Her intense practices and inadequate nutrition led to a physical and emotional breaking point. Determined to excel, Bobby exceeded her coach's training regimens without adjusting her food intake, resulting in frail bones and unexpected fractures. Despite her young age and apparent fitness, she was diagnosed with osteoporosis and now out of Olympic contention, shocking her and her family.

Now in recovery, she supports the #TRAINBRAVE campaign to raise awareness about over-training and inadequate nutrition in sports. Bobby emphasizes the importance of listening to others and not succumbing to the pressure to push oneself constantly. She gradually strengthens her bones through cycling training and intends to return to running. Her ultimate goal is to represent her country at the Olympics someday.

Nutrition's Role

To achieve peak bone mass, adequate nutrition and physical activity are essential. Studies have shown that insufficient intake of nutrients such as calcium and vitamin D during growth can negatively affect bone mass development in children. Eating disorders like anorexia nervosa can also directly impact bone mass due to severe nutrient deficiency, reducing bone formation and increasing bone resorption. Even short-term fasting can cause a marked decrease in bone formation markers in young and healthy individuals.

It is crucial to emphasize the significance of achieving peak bone mass during adolescence, which can delay the onset of osteoporosis by up to 13 years and reduce the risk of osteoporotic fractures later in life. While bone loss naturally occurs after age 40, adults can prevent severe bone loss and osteoporosis by maintaining a balanced diet and regular exercise.

Recent research has demonstrated that following a Mediterranean diet can lower the risk of hip fractures in postmenopausal women. This diet emphasizes consuming fish, vegetables, fruits, whole grains, legumes, nuts, seeds, and olive oil while limiting meat, cheese, and sweets. Thus, focusing on overall healthy eating habits is more beneficial for supporting bone health than single nutrient intake.

Calcium

Calcium is critical for building strong bones and various bodily functions such as muscle contraction, nerve impulse transmission, immune system function, and regulating blood pressure. Our bodies store most of the calcium in our bones, and a lack of calcium in our diet can weaken them. While supplements are necessary, obtaining the recommended daily amount of calcium from food sources is advised. Dairy products are a popular source, but it's better to include other foods such as leafy green vegetables, fish, beans, nuts, and seeds. Pairing calcium-rich foods with vitamin D sources can enhance calcium absorption.

Vitamin D and Sunlight

Adequate vitamin D is essential for healthy bones, which we obtain through safe sun exposure or supplements. The suggested average daily intake of vitamin D for seniors is 600-800 IU (international units). Some suggest it should be 1000 IU or more if you are over 70 or have osteoporosis.

Similarly, magnesium is also paramount for bone health as it enhances calcium absorption. Including magnesium-rich foods like spinach, seeds, beans, quinoa, and nuts in your diet can help maintain healthy magnesium levels. The recommended daily intake of magnesium is between 400 and 800 mg.

Vitamin K

Vitamin K is crucial for bone health, reducing osteoporosis and fractures. Additionally, supplementing with vitamin K2 improves bone density and fracture risk in postmenopausal women. It aids calcium absorption, prevents accumulation in organs and arteries, and activates a protein called osteocalcin, which binds calcium to bones. Dietary sources of vitamin K2 include meat, poultry, eggs, Brie, Gouda, and natto (a Japanese food derived from soybeans). Plant-based proteins like beans, legumes, nuts, seeds, and soy also benefit bone health, especially when combined with high-quality animal proteins.

Nutrition for Balance

Salt

Salt, AKA sodium chloride, is a necessary nutrient for our bodies. Some say that pink Himalayan and Celtic Sea varieties are best because they contain more minerals and are less processed than typical table salt. That said, excessive consumption is typical (for any variety) due to our love for salt's coveted flavor. Health Canada suggests a maximum daily intake of 2300 mg of sodium and an adequate intake of less than 1500 mg. Choosing whole foods and cooking at home can help manage sodium intake. Be cautious of high-sodium foods like canned soups, packaged meals, pickled foods, deli meats, and salty snacks. Reading labels is essential, aiming for 5% DV (daily value) or less for a bit of salt and 15% DV or more for a lot. "Sodium-free" foods have less than 5 mg per serving, while "less sodium" indicates a 25% reduction. Some antacids may also contain high sodium levels.

Tyramine

Tyramine is an amino acid that regulates blood pressure. However, consuming foods high in tyramine can trigger vestibular migraine for some individuals. Foods that are aged or fermented tend to be particularly rich in tyramine. These include strong or aged cheeses, smoked, processed, or cured meats, and fish, Asian-style sauces like soy sauce, fish sauce, miso, and teriyaki sauce, as well as dried or overripe fruits, meat tenderizers, Marmite®, and brewer's yeast. Other sources of tyramine include soybeans, snow peas, broad beans, and nuts. Therefore, individuals sensitive to tyramine must be aware of these foods and limit their consumption to prevent migraine attacks.

Nitrates and Nitrites

Specific individuals may have elevated levels of gut microbes that convert nitrates found in food into by-products of nitric oxide, potentially triggering vestibular migraines. In addition, consuming foods containing nitrites may have a similar effect. Foods abundant in nitrates/nitrites include cured meats, chocolate, and wine.

Gluten

About 25% of individuals with celiac disease may develop autonomic neuropathy, leading to occasional vertigo, syncope, and nausea. In addition, research indicates a potential link between gluten sensitivity and vestibular migraine. While the evidence is limited, some studies suggest a gluten-free diet may alleviate imbalances in individuals with Ménière's disease. Gluten-containing foods include barley, bulgur, couscous, durum, einkorn, emmer, faro, kamut, malt, rye, semolina, spelt, triticale (a flour), wheat, wheat bran, wheat germ, and wheat starch. It's worth noting that most commercially available oats may contain small amounts of wheat or barley, and many packaged foods contain gluten, so carefully reading labels is essential.

Aspartame

Some people may experience adverse effects on their inner ear, such as nausea, headaches, dizziness (spinning feeling), ear ringing, and hearing loss due to consuming the artificial sweetener known as aspartame. However, these symptoms are usually temporary and disappear once aspartame is removed from one's diet.

MSG

Monosodium glutamate (MSG), a flavor enhancer, can cause headaches and dizziness in specific individuals when consumed as an ingredient in food. It is commonly found in various canned foods, so people sensitive to MSG should read product labels carefully. Additionally, MSG is stereotypically linked to Asian restaurants and their cuisine.

A Note on Caffeine and Alcohol

Consuming caffeine and alcohol may exacerbate their symptoms for those with dizziness and balance issues. If you suspect these substances may contribute to your symptoms, consider avoiding them to determine if your condition improves. Although caffeinated drinks may mildly increase urination, they do not elevate the risk of dehydration. However, caffeine can raise cortisol (a stress hormone) levels by more than twice the average amount, potentially contributing to stress. Other things to consider:

- Avoid caffeine if you are recovering from a concussion.
- In addition to coffee, caffeine is present in tea, chocolate, and yerba mate (a South American tea). In addition, soft drinks flavored with the kola nut or guarana (a plant native to the Amazon) may contain it.
- According to The Vestibular Disorders Association, alcohol can negatively impact the inner ear (and balance) by modifying the volume and composition of its fluid.

Eating for Better Bones and Balance

Maintaining a healthy diet is critical for overall well-being, regardless of whether you experience joint pain or imbalance. Moreover, incorporating certain foods into your diet promotes bone and joint health. Here are some essential nutrients and their food sources to consider:

- Omega-3 fatty acids: Omega-3s combat inflammation and support heart health. Managing inflammation is essential for reducing pain and improving functionality, especially for individuals with rheumatoid arthritis. Fatty fish like salmon, sardines, tuna, mackerel, and herring are excellent sources of omega-3s. Additionally, flaxseeds, walnuts, and edamame contain these beneficial fatty acids.
- Calcium is crucial in maintaining strong bones, muscle control, and blood circulation. Since our bodies do not produce calcium naturally, acquiring it through our diet is essential. While dairy products are commonly associated with calcium intake, non-dairy alternatives are also available. Dairy options include milk, cheese, and yogurt. In contrast, non-dairy sources include fortified cereals, edamame, dark leafy greens like kale and spinach, and enriched soy or almond milk.

- Vitamin D: Vitamin D aids in efficiently absorbing calcium from food. While sunlight exposure allows our bodies to produce vitamin D, it is advisable to obtain it through dietary sources or supplements to avoid excessive sunlight. Fatty fish, fortified milk, fortified orange juice, egg yolks, and fortified cereals are excellent sources of vitamin D.

- Vitamin C: Vitamin C helps reduce the risk of inflammatory arthritis and supports healthy joints. Oranges, grapefruits, limes, strawberries, mangos, pineapple, and bell peppers are excellent sources of vitamin C.

- Anthocyanins: In red and purple fruits, anthocyanins are potent antioxidants that help reduce inflammation. Cherries, strawberries, raspberries, blueberries, and blackberries are rich in anthocyanins.

- Polyphenols: Polyphenols, a group of antioxidants, have shown promise in reducing joint inflammation and preserving cartilage. Green, black, oolong, and white teas are excellent sources of polyphenols, with matcha containing exceptionally high concentrations.

- Sulforaphane: Sulforaphane protects joint cartilage and alleviates inflammation associated with osteoarthritis. Cruciferous vegetables like broccoli, Brussels sprouts, cabbage, cauliflower, and kale are abundant sources of sulforaphane.

- Diallyl disulfide: Garlic, onions, and leeks, belonging to the allium family, are rich sources of diallyl disulfide. Incorporating these aromatic ingredients into your meals may provide protective effects against early signs of osteoarthritis.

A Magic Elixir: Bone Broth

In the world of nutrition, bone broth is almost like a panacea. Of course, it does not cure all ailments, but it packs so much great nutrition that you should consider having some of it in your diet.

How does it benefit bone health? Well, there needs to be a detailed study on the correlation between consuming bone broth and improved bone health. However, what we do know is that bone broth contains a lot of nutrients that help with our bone health, such as:

- Collagen: Makes up about 1/3 of the protein in our bodies, and it also serves as the main component of our bones, tendons, skin, cartilage, and ligament. Our bodies need it to repair cells and tissues.

- Gelatin: Contains amino acids and helps in digestive, joint, and skin health, among other benefits.

- Glycosaminoglycans: GAGs, for short, support and maintain collagen and elastin to retain their moisture. They also work with other proteins to produce lubrication (synovial fluid) for our joints.

- Glycine: Found in collagen, this amino acid is an essential neurotransmitter in the nervous system and can dampen inflammation, protect the liver, and promote better sleep, among other benefits.

- Proline: Also found in collagen, it works with glycine to create collagen. It also promotes wound healing.

- Glutamine: Found in human blood, skeletal muscles, and collagen. It is a fuel source for the cells that line our intestines.

- Assorted minerals: Copper, iron, manganese, magnesium, phosphorus, calcium, sodium, zinc, etc. All of them are beneficial to our bones.

Other Foods That Help Bones

Do none of the above strike your fancy, or are you looking to improve your bone health further? Consider the following:

Coconut Oil

Studies show that virgin coconut oil (VCO) effectively improves bone structure and helps prevent bone loss in an animal model of osteoporosis. Furthermore, the observed beneficial effects on bone microarchitecture are believed to be associated with the high levels of polyphenols found in VCO, which possess potent antioxidant properties. Therefore, VCO holds potential as an exciting approach to counteract the accelerated bone loss in osteoporosis, with particular relevance for postmenopausal women.

Does it have to be virgin coconut oil? Yes, because regular coconut oil goes through a refining process where it loses its antioxidants. Ideally, get organic VCO to get the bone-building benefits and more.

Blackberries

The nutritional profile of blackberries is truly impressive, offering a range of essential minerals, vitamins, antioxidants, and other beneficial nutrients. Incorporating blackberries in your diet provides various antioxidants, protecting against free radicals, reducing inflammation, and supporting multiple aspects of bone health.

By incorporating blackberries into your meals and snacks, you can enjoy their delicious taste while reaping their benefits for your overall well-being, including bone health.

What is Astaxanthin?

One of the global leaders, including independent studies and bone health supplement manufacturing for seniors, is a company called AlgaeCal. One of their board members, Dr. Loren Fishman, recently wrote an article about the many benefits of Astaxanthin. As fancy as the name sounds, it's a naturally occurring nutrient found in microalgae, and it produces red coloring in sea creatures like krill, salmon, and shellfish. Astaxanthin is touted with significant benefits like improving inflammation, bones and joints, vision, skin, circulation, immune response, recovery, endurance, circulation, and recovery. As you can see, this little guy packs a big punch. While there's no set recommendation for quantity for these benefits, AlgaeCal recommends 6-8 mg per day to obtain the benefits of this nutrient. I've placed a link to the article in the references under this chapter if you want to read more about it.

Hydration's Role

Water is essential for the proper functioning of our cells, tissues, bones, and organs. It goes beyond regulating body temperature and helps with moisture, digestion, and waste elimination. For example, water is a crucial component of bones, alongside apatite mineral and collagen protein, directly affecting their strength, density, and remodeling ability.

Maintaining proper hydration is vital for strong and healthy bones. Dehydration can increase the release of cortisol and other stress hormones, leading to accelerated bone loss. Insufficient fluid intake also impairs kidney function, affecting the pH balance needed for preserving bone mass. In addition, dehydration allows toxins to accumulate, creating an acidic environment that harms bone health.

Daily water intake recommendations vary, influenced by age, activity level, climate, and overall health. Yet it's essential to prioritize adequate hydration to support optimal bone health.

With this in mind, let's quickly explore some fruits and veggies with the highest water content. These fruits and vegetables provide hydration and various bone-essential nutrients and antioxidants, contributing to overall health.

It is recommended to choose organically grown options, particularly for any items on the "Dirty Dozen" list, which can change from year to year. The Dirty Dozen list reveals twelve non-organic fruits and veggies that typically contain the highest pesticide residue. So if you're choosing any of these foods for hydration purposes, it's better to get organics if they're on that list. The list is published annually by the Environmental Working Group (EWG), which you can easily see by Googling "Dirty Dozen." The EWG also makes a list called the "Clean Fifteen." If you're interested in seeing both of these lists, please check the references at the back of the book under this chapter heading. Here are the best hydration foods:

- Celery: With 95.43% water, celery is rich in bone-essential nutrients and phytonutrients that lower blood pressure. It is also a good source of fiber.
- Radish: Radish contains 95.27% water and is packed with bone-smart Vitamin C and other essential nutrients.
- Cucumber: Cucumber, with 95.23% water, is technically a fruit high in Vitamin K and silica, contributing to bone strength.
- Zucchini: With 94.79% water, zucchini is rich in Vitamin C and flavonoid antioxidants that help slow aging and protect against bone loss.
- Tomato: Tomatoes contain 94.5% water and are nutritional powerhouses, rich in vitamins and antioxidants, including lycopene, which stimulates bone-building cells.
- Bell Peppers: Bell peppers have 93.89% water content and are high in potassium and Vitamin C, essential for maintaining pH levels and bone health.
- Cabbage: With 92.18% water, cabbage is rich in Vitamins C and K and contains inflammation-fighting phytonutrients and antioxidants.
- Cauliflower: Cauliflower, with 92.07% water, is a source of Vitamin C and antioxidants, and it helps release toxins from the body.
- Grapefruit: Grapefruit contains 91.56% water and is high in Vitamin C and antioxidants that slow down bone loss and decrease the risk of kidney stones.

- Watermelon: With 91.45% water, watermelon is hydrating and rich in carotenoids, Vitamins A and C, and lycopene, which supports bone health.
- Spinach: Spinach has 91.4% water and is a calcium-rich leafy green vegetable with potassium, Vitamin K, and other bone-friendly minerals.
- Strawberries: Strawberries contain 90.95% water and are a valuable source of Vitamin C, manganese, and antioxidants that fight free radicals.
- Cantaloupe: Cantaloupe, with 90.15% water, is hydrating and rich in Vitamin C, potassium, and beta-carotene, an antioxidant that helps combat free radicals.

A Gut Feeling

Maintaining a healthy gut is essential for improving bone health and overall well-being. The human body harbors a vast array of microorganisms known as the human microbiota, which reside in various parts such as the skin, nose, mouth, and, most significantly, the gut.

If you're just now learning about these microorganisms, this might sound unsettling. But they are not worrisome. Their main role is to perform vital functions crucial for human survival. The gut, which contains a significant portion of these microbes, forms the gut microbiome or gut microflora.

Contrary to common belief, the microbiome has a broader impact than just digestion, affecting many things like immunity, nutrition, diseases, and behavior. Extensive research has been conducted on this topic, revealing a strong connection between an imbalanced gut microbiome and various conditions, including heart disease, diabetes, obesity, asthma, cancer, eczema, and, yes, bone health.

Studies show that modulation of the gut and its microbiome can influence bone density and strength. Exciting new evidence suggests that consuming probiotics may have a favorable effect in reducing the risk of osteoporosis. This data highlights the significant role that optimal gut health plays in preventing bone conditions and other related health issues.

To reap the benefits of these microbes, adopting healthy eating habits and engaging in regular exercise is crucial for our immune system. This optimizes the functionality of the gut microbiome, which serves as the body's second gene pool. These microorganisms play a role in immune function, nutrient absorption, and various activities of host cells, including those related to bone health. They indirectly affect bone metabolism by influencing osteoblasts and osteoclasts, crucial for maintaining the balance between bone formation and resorption. Additionally, they regulate growth factors, impact bone immune status, and affect the metabolism of important substances like serotonin, cortisol, and sex hormones, thus influencing bone health. Modifying the intestinal microbiota through probiotics and diet can potentially aid in treating bone diseases.

Nutrition Questionnaire

Below is a short questionnaire I've compiled to help determine whether you are doing a good job staying healthy and getting the proper nutrients. Use this as no more than a quick litmus test. If you check fewer than 50% of these, you should put exercise and better nutritional solutions at the tippy top of your to-do list.

___I thoroughly understand the number of calories I should consume daily.

___I regularly set short-term goals and review them consistently.

___I proactively plan my meals and snacks in advance.

___I incorporate exercise or physical activity into my daily routine.

___I prioritize strength training sessions two or three times per week.

___I stay adequately hydrated by drinking eight glasses of water daily.

___I strive to consume at least five servings of fruits and vegetables daily.

___I establish regular mealtimes to promote a consistent eating schedule.

___I consciously focus on my meals, avoiding distractions like watching TV.

___I practice mindful eating by chewing my food slowly and thoroughly.

___I take breaks between bites by setting down my silverware.

___I dedicate a minimum of 20 minutes to each meal, allowing time for enjoyment.

___After eating, I take the opportunity to relax or go for a brisk walk.

___I keep a variety of low-fat, low-calorie snacks available for healthy choices.

___I refrain from nibbling while engaged in cooking or cleaning activities.

___I limit my intake of high-fat foods such as rich desserts, sauces, and gravies.

___I consistently create and adhere to a shopping list, avoiding impulse purchases.

___I avoid shopping while hungry or excessively stressed.

___I carefully read food labels to enhance my awareness of nutritional content.

___I can maintain my meal plan even when dining out.

___I actively increase my walking frequency and duration.

___I opt for taking the stairs instead of using elevators whenever feasible.

___I feel self-assured and in control of both my diet and my body.

___I weigh myself no more than once weekly to track my progress effectively.

___I engage in de-stressing exercises to manage and overcome urges to overeat.

___I reward myself for accomplishing short-term goals as positive reinforcement.

___I utilize positive self-talk to sustain my motivation and focus.

___I consistently maintain reasonable portion sizes to support my health goals.

___I seek alternative indoor exercises when outdoor weather conditions are unfavorable.

___I have a clear understanding of my reasons and motivations for weight loss.

___I possess confidence in my abilities and strive to achieve goals.

Chapter Summary

- Good nutrition is essential because your body's functions, specifically balance, require it to maintain itself. The same applies to the muscles and bones that keep you standing straight.

- Calcium, vitamin D, K, coconut oil, blackberries, and foods with high water content are some things you should consider incorporating into your diet. Sugar, salt, and gluten are things you should moderate.

- There are some amazing foods and nutrients that can improve our balance and bones. One of these foods is bone broth, which is incredibly potent for promoting bone health as it contains all the nutrients your bones need to stay healthy.

- Astaxanthin is a super nutrient that improves inflammation, bones and joints, vision, skin, circulation, immune response, recovery, endurance, circulation, and recovery

- We must maintain good gut health to get the most from our food.

- We should consistently keep our nutrition in check to achieve optimal bone and balance performance.

7

OVERCOMING BARRIERS TO EXERCISE

"The longer I live, the more beautiful life becomes."
– Frank Lloyd Wright

———

When I was a freshman in college, I called my dad near the end of the school term with tears in my eyes. I'd taken on some major lumps that year, which made me rethink my choice of schools. I was struggling academically while trying to make the wrestling team and balance the demands of a music degree. Without hesitation, my dad told me he was ok with me changing schools. He could tell that I was almost broken mentally and physically, and it hurt him to see me like that. However, he patiently asked me one simple question that I'll always remember. He said, "Matt, what do you really want to accomplish in the next few years"? When I answered this question, I knew the decision that I needed to make.

That question removed a barrier, and that barrier was that I had an unclear goal. I knew I wanted to compete in the sport of wrestling and receive the best degree possible. But I hadn't yet defined what that looked like. The question produced clarity of goals which, consequently, motivated me to make the decision. Once I more clearly defined what I wanted, it made it more apparent that I needed to stay at that school.

This is just one example of removing a "barrier" to an objective. Let's take a moment to examine some other specific barriers we may face and how we can remove them.

Removing Barriers

Chapters 1-6 provided us with a bit of academic guidance in the pursuit of better balance and bones. However, none of that knowledge matters if we cannot or do not put it into practice. Let's look at some of the things that might keep us from implementing the healthy and fit lifestyle that we truly desire. Here are some common barriers that can hinder our progress:

- Insufficient tools: Lack of access to or availability of necessary tools, technologies, or resources can impede our progress. With the right tools, it can be easier to achieve desired outcomes efficiently.

- Lack of goals: It becomes easier to establish a sense of direction and purpose with clear goals or objectives. Goals provide a framework for progress and help prioritize efforts and resources.

- Lack of knowledge: Inadequate knowledge or information about a particular subject or process can limit progress. It's essential to continually learn and adapt to new information to overcome obstacles and make informed decisions.

- Laziness: Lack of motivation, discipline, or effort can hinder our progress. Procrastination, complacency, or a reluctance to act can prevent individuals or teams from moving forward.

- Lack of help/accountability: Progress can be impeded when there is a lack of support or assistance from others. Sometimes, we may struggle to accomplish tasks or overcome challenges without guidance, mentorship, or accountability.

- Lack of focus: Lack of concentration or the inability to prioritize effectively can lead to a lack of progress. Without a clear focus on the most important tasks or objectives, our efforts may be scattered or inefficiently allocated.

- Lack of self-confidence or self-worth. Without believing that we can accomplish new things, we will lack the desire to move ahead. We must become the Little Engine That Could.

- Lack of discipline. This is probably the hardest yet most rewarding barrier to eliminate. If we can become more disciplined, it even trumps motivation and many of the other barriers. It may be the most important barrier of all to eliminate.

Technique

Every fitness expert agrees that the quality of your reps is more important than their quantity. Simply put, ten good pushups are better than 100 pushups with improper form. In Chapter 5, we dove into the subject of posture and how it relates to balance. In this section, we will discuss how posture applies to our form when exercising and how we can get the most from our workouts by applying this knowledge. Having good form removes a barrier to exercise.

Form and Posture

"Stand up straight." We've heard this all the time. It's advice that holds true, and it's advice that my mom gave me and her mother before her. "Head up and shoulders back," her mom used to say to her.

As we've discussed, good posture is essential for maintaining balance, as it aligns your body and centers your weight over your feet. This promotes correct form during exercise, reduces the risk of injuries and maximizes gains, and enhances performance in various sports and activities such as tennis, golf, running, dancing, skiing, and more.

Even if you're not particularly active, having good balance is still beneficial. Daily tasks like walking across a room or reaching up into your kitchen cupboards require stability and equilibrium. Rising from a chair, climbing stairs, carrying objects, and even turning to look behind you all rely on having a solid sense of balance.

Poor posture is not merely a bad habit; it can also be caused by physical factors, including:

- Inflexible muscles that limit our range of motion. For example, tight hip muscles can pull our upper body forward, disrupting our posture. In contrast, tight chest muscles can pull our shoulders forward.
- Muscle weakness affects our balance in various ways. The core muscles, including those in our back, sides, pelvis, and buttocks, are a solid link between our upper and lower body. Weak core muscles contribute to slumping, throwing our body off balance. Similarly, strong lower leg muscles help stabilize us when standing.

The good news is that we can improve our posture through simple exercises. Balance-specific workouts target posture and balance issues by strengthening the relevant muscle groups and stretching tight areas. Regularly checking our posture in the mirror before and during balance exercises can also help us make the most out of our regular workout routine. Additionally, enhancing our core strength and flexibility can lead to noticeable improvements in our posture within just a few weeks.

So, what does good posture entail while exercising?

- Keeping your chin parallel to the floor.
- Maintaining even shoulders by rolling them up, back, and down.
- Keep your spine neutral without excessive arching or flexing of the lower back.
- Allowing your arms to hang naturally at your sides with straight and even elbows.
- Engaging your abdominal muscles to brace your core.
- Ensuring your hips and knees are even and not misaligned or crooked.
- Pointing your knees straight ahead.
- Equal weight distribution.

We should usually keep our chin parallel to the floor when seated, maintain even heights for our shoulders, hips, and knees, and ensure that our knees and feet point straight ahead. There are exceptions to the rule, but this usually applies to all exercises.

Breathing

Proper breathing is key to any exercise, impacting performance and fitness. Despite being a vital bodily function, many overlook it during workouts. It's important to know the right way to breathe for each activity. For instance, during bicep curls, resisting the urge to hold your breath is crucial. Good posture, controlled movement, and intentional breathing are essential for maintaining proper exercise form. Correct breathing offers numerous benefits, such as:

- Strengthening the diaphragm and the nervous system.
- Relaxing the muscles in your neck and shoulders.
- Enhancing your body's ability to endure intense exercise.
- Increasing oxygen supply to the working muscles.
- Reducing blood pressure and anxiety.
- Strengthening respiratory muscles and improving endurance.
- Prolonging exercise duration and reducing feelings of fatigue.
- Enhancing body stability, such as a tightened core.
- Increasing nitric oxide levels relaxes arteries and promotes blood flow.

Proper breathing during exercise is easier initially but becomes more challenging with fatigue. Belly breathing allows the lungs to expand downward, improving circulation in the lower one-third of the lungs. Shallow breathing, also called chest breathing, fills only the upper one-third of the lungs and hampers circulation. Chest breathing requires more energy and frequent breaths. To identify your breathing type, try the exercise mentioned below:

- Put one hand on your stomach and the other on your chest.
- Inhale and observe the movement under your hands.
- If only the hand on your chest moves, you're utilizing chest breathing.
- If only the hand on your belly moves, you're utilizing belly breathing.
- If both hands move, it indicates belly breathing, meaning you're taking deep enough breaths to fill your lungs. This is also acceptable as the goal is first to fill the belly, followed by the chest.

Lastly, it's important to avoid holding your breath while exercising. Although it's a common instinct during challenging workouts, this can result in injury. Always breathe when exercising!

Visualization

Proper mental preparation before an intense workout is beneficial. For example, visualizing workout goals can even help us increase muscle engagement and enhance sensations. You can either do it before you start working out or during the session prior to an exercise.

If you want mental prep before your session, spend just a few minutes visualizing. The preparation length and depth are a matter of personal preference. Consider what might work best for you, and then experiment with some of the following:

- Imagine completing your workout goals for that session.
- Engage your senses, imagining your gym environment and immersing yourself in the moment.
- Visualize flawless execution of each exercise, focusing on breathing and incorporating details.
- Imagine the post-workout sensations of soreness, accomplishment, and exertion.

- Before beginning an exercise, imagine the weight's heaviness and the strain on your muscles.
- Consider how you will feel mentally after you've accomplished a workout.
- After your visualization happens, take immediate action.

One simple way to start putting this into practice is before you get out of bed in the morning. Take a few moments before you start your day and practice breathing. Visualize good posture, stretching and even some of the exercises you will do that day.

We can overcome mental obstacles and improve our performance by programming our minds. It is essential to set realistic expectations, however. Avoid creating unrealistic scenarios driven by ego. Focus on what you can realistically accomplish. Visualization requires experimentation, practice, and concentration, so be patient if results don't come immediately.

Hydration

We discussed hydration in Chapter 6, but it's so important that I need to mention it here. Staying hydrated is crucial for optimal bodily function. Insufficient fluid intake can have various adverse effects, such as:

- Body temperature and heart rate may rise as your body struggles to regulate heat.
- Fatigue can set in, leading to increased tiredness.
- Impaired cognitive abilities, motor control, decision-making, and concentration may occur.
- Slowed bodily functions, including gastric emptying, can cause discomfort.
- Performance in sports or exercise may suffer, particularly in hot conditions when dehydrated.

Staying hydrated during exercise is vital for optimal performance. To replenish lost fluids and prevent heat stress, always drink water while being physically active. This helps maintain concentration, endurance, and normal bodily function. Water is the ideal choice as it is natural, easily accessible, and calorie-free. Take sips both during and after your workout and aim to drink approximately 1.5 times the amount of fluid you lost. And don't chug it all at once; spread it out over several hours, starting at the top of your routine.

Mental Tools

On top of knowing what workouts to pursue, we also need to have a clear goal. You need to know what the results look like. "Losing weight" and "improving my balance" are good but not specific enough. It would help if you had clear goals.

Clear Cut Goals

Pursuing goals is essential to being human, providing meaning, purpose, and happiness. Whether big or small, setting goals guide us, sparks our enthusiasm, and enhances engagement. Aristotle's wisdom holds even today: starting well is halfway to success. Effective goal setting increases our chances of achievement and brings fulfillment. Here's how to begin:

- Choose a goal that genuinely interests and excites you, driven by your desires.
- Write down your goals with specific details, timelines, and indicators of success.
- Share your goals with someone you trust to strengthen your commitment.
- Break down big goals into smaller milestones, adding clarity and a sense of accomplishment.
- Plan the first step towards your goal, even if unsure, and continue mapping subsequent steps.
- Stay persistent and adapt as needed, seeking input from others for new perspectives.
- Celebrate achievements, express gratitude, and reflect on the journey's positive aspects.
- Embrace pursuing goals to enrich and fulfill your life's journey.

Proper Motivation

Motivation propels us towards goals, influenced by desire, gains, losses, and expectations. It aids problem-solving, habit change, and coping with challenges. Starting can be really tough sometimes, but motivation follows action, and overcoming resistance is vital.

Motivation can be tricky too. Sometimes it's as easy as being determined enough to fit into our favorite dress or suit for an upcoming wedding. Or, perhaps we want to fit into a new bathing suit on our next trip to the beach. But if we don't have those kinds of occasions in our sights, we often need help discovering something that's going to push us toward our objectives.

Also, finding motivation when "slumping" can be challenging, especially during change. We may have been consistently motivated for months, and yet sometimes that consistency can (and will) wain. It's human nature and is completely normal. But never worry if you get into a funk. Just pull out these handy tips for motivation to help if (and when) you're struggling.

- Set a specific and achievable goal for yourself.
- Find the "why" (the reason) you have a particular goal and write it down.
- Set a timeframe for achieving the goal, such as one week or month.
- Break down your goal into small, manageable tasks daily and weekly.
- Set reminders or create a schedule to ensure consistent progress.
- Reach out to family and friends for support. Their support can be invaluable in keeping you motivated and accountable towards your goals.

To stay on track and maintain motivation toward your goal, consider the following strategies:

- Incorporate your goal into your daily routine using tools like a diary, calendar, or mobile app for reminders. This keeps goals at the forefront of your mind and ensures progress.
- Practice positive self-talk, especially when managing depression or anxiety. Replace negative thoughts like "I can't" with positive affirmations such as "I can try." This shift in mindset promotes self-belief and resilience.
- Cultivate mindfulness to stay relaxed and focused. Mindfulness techniques, such as meditation or deep breathing exercises, help manage stress and distractions.
- Reward yourself upon completing a goal. Celebrating milestones reinforces progress and provides a sense of accomplishment. This can be as simple as treating yourself to a yummy healthy snack or even a trip to the outlet malls for some bargains.

To sustain motivation throughout your journey, try the following strategies:

- Regularly review your goals and track progress. Observing tangible progress is a powerful motivator that boosts self-esteem and keeps you engaged.

- Continually set new goals. Consider what you want to achieve in the coming weeks, months, and years.

- Maintain momentum by establishing a routine. Developing a new habit typically takes around two months. Sticking to a routine will make your goal-related actions more automatic.

- Seek guidance from individuals experienced in the habit or area you wish to change.

- Spend time with people who encourage you. Positive friends and family members contribute to a supportive environment and enhance your positive self-talk.

- Make exercise a daily goal to improve your mental health. Physical activity has numerous mental and emotional benefits, including increased motivation and well-being.

What to do if you lose motivation. Experiencing setbacks or temporary loss of motivation is not abnormal. To regain your motivation, consider the following steps:

- Break down your goal into smaller, more achievable bites. Adjusting your approach can help regain focus and enthusiasm.

- Remind yourself "why" you wanted to pursue the goal in the first place. Reconnecting with your initial motivations can reignite your passion and drive.

- Seek motivation from external sources. Find inspiration by reading books, talking to a mentor, or engaging with friends and family who have achieved similar goals. Learning from their experiences and successes can renew your motivation.

- Sometimes, taking a break and starting afresh is necessary. Allow yourself time to recharge and reassess your goals.

Accountability

One of the most effective approaches to achieving your fitness goals is establishing personal accountability for your actions. In the realm of fitness, accountability refers to taking responsibility for your dietary choices, exercise routines, and progress toward your fitness objectives. Whether you're trying to lose weight, adopt healthier eating habits, or prepare for a significant race, incorporating accountability into your fitness program can work wonders. For example, sharing a challenge with a friend increases the chance of completion to 65%, but committing to meet (and work) with someone in person raises it to 95%. To achieve long-term success in your fitness journey, maintaining accountability is extremely beneficial.

Patience

From there, you need to be patient. Patience is key. While no one really knows how long the pyramids took to build, they were not built overnight, and no enduring civilizations ever rose within a day. And even though we're not building physical cities here, aren't our bodies and minds just as important, if not more? Therefore, we need to understand that we're going to make mistakes and fall down on occasion. There is no better teacher than failure. But having the patience to know that we can still succeed despite our failures makes all the difference.

Physical Tools

- A chair: A chair is a versatile tool that enhances home workouts by providing support and stability. It enables targeting of the entire body, including the lower and upper body, for calorie burning, core strengthening, and muscle building. Chairs are particularly beneficial for individuals with mobility and balance issues, offering additional support. They are suitable for seated stretches and provide a stable base for various movements.

- A yoga mat: A yoga mat or a carpeted floor is essential for comfortable and safe workouts. Exercising on a hard surface can lead to discomfort and potential injuries. A yoga mat provides cushioning during exercise and prevents the need to lie on a dirty floor while sweating. Additionally, yoga mats offer an extra layer of protection, which is especially important for individuals with sensitive joints. The stability provided by a mat also reduces the risk of slipping and falling, particularly during complex exercises.

- Towel: Believe it or not, towels can play an important role in workouts beyond their obvious use. They act as a protective barrier against germs and keep us cool and our hands dry during exercise. When used creatively, towels can target various muscle groups, such as shoulders, arms, lats, and legs. They can be transformed into resistance bands by twisting them into a rope-like shape. Rolled-up towels provide additional support during floor exercises and can replace cushions like wedges and bolsters.

- Dumbbells: Light weights, such as 1-5 lbs. dumbbells, are valuable tools for building muscle and improving endurance. Incorporating light weights into workouts helps define muscles and enhance joint functionality. Additionally, using weights allows us to burn calories and engage in sustainable workout routines that can be maintained over a long period of time. A full water bottle or a can of veggies can also do the trick if you don't want to purchase dumbbells.

- Clothing: Wear loose-fitting and breathable clothes along with supportive shoes. Do not use just socks, and do not go barefoot. Neither provides enough support and may cause shin splints. Additionally, socks can slip if using yoga mats. For your attire, consider fabrics such as cotton, bamboo, nylon, and polyester that offer comfort and breathability. Choose clothing that enhances your performance and makes you feel comfortable and remind yourself that you don't need to look fashionable. Comfort is key when exercising.

Optional:

- Consider investing in foam rollers, resistance bands, a bench, a broomstick/dowel, and an exercise ball.

- Foam rollers are essential for self-myofascial release (SMR), which is basically a "self-massage" technique. Rollers can provide relief for lower back pain and shoulder soreness during floor exercises. And rolling over muscles can promote relaxation, improve blood flow, and massage tight calf muscles.

- Resistance bands are an affordable, safe, and portable tool that allows you to build muscle and burn calories. They provide a versatile way to target almost every muscle in your body, with varying resistance levels based on band thickness.

- Benches are highly recommended for resistance workouts as they offer essential support. They enhance the quality of your exercises and allow for a broader range of movements, making them a valuable addition to any home gym setup.

- Exercise balls are particularly effective for strengthening core muscles and improving balance, flexibility, and coordination. They also contribute to better posture, providing added stability during your workouts.

Chapter Summary

- To maximize the effectiveness of your workouts, you must focus on good form before completing the required repetition number for that workout. The reason is that good form engages the right muscles and takes you through the proper motion and motion range, delivering the desired result. The improper form may lead to injuries. So, quality over quantity.

- It also helps to visualize yourself going through your workout. It is proven that doing so can help you push through.

- Hydration is also essential. You will sweat when you exercise, so you need to replenish the lost fluid.

- You must also have a suite of mental tools to help you stay on track. You need to have clear goals to know where you are heading. It would be best if you were also motivated to maintain your new lifestyle. Consider having a system of accountability in the form of journaling or having a partner to remind you of what you are working toward. Finally, it would be best to have patience because fitness does not occur overnight.

PART TWO

EXERCISES & WORKOUTS FOR BALANCE,
BONES, AND POSTURE

8

THE 64 EXERCISES

"I think self-discipline is something. It's like a muscle.
The more you exercise it, the stronger it gets."
– Daniel Goldstein

———————

Throughout the first part of this book, we've talked about the academic and theoretical sides of bettering our balance, bones, and posture. We've mentioned all the adjustments we can and should make in our habits to improve our health in these three critical categories. And now, it is time to jump into the second part of the book, the hands-on side…the really fun part, the exercises and workouts!

Form and Function

As we jump in, I must tell you that there are some counterproductive ways to exercise, especially when lifting weights. And they can lead to negative results, harm joints, tear muscles, and slow recovery or preventative maintenance processes. So, as mentioned in Chapter 7, form, posture, and breathing are critical.

Your form should match the illustrations as best as possible, knowing that these will always be a work in progress. As I write this book, I also plan to include video examples of the form as supplements to the illustrations.

Generally, movement should be fluid and steady with no erratic or jerky motions. Please note that many of these exercises can be done seated or standing. Do not hold your breath. Breathing should be slow, steady, and relaxed throughout the exercises.

Muscle Groups

What muscle groups are best to work out together and why?

Our muscles need both exercise and rest to function well. For this reason, it's sometimes a good idea to work out specific muscle groups together as we let others rest. When we do this, we give our muscles enough recovery time.

There's also the "whole body" approach, where the 2-3 times you exercise per week involves using exercises that hit all the muscle groups simultaneously. Both systems work, and both have pros and cons. For the purposes of this book, we will take a "whole body" approach. Why should we exercise specific muscle groups together?

The whole point of resistance training is to improve the strength of specific muscles through targeted exercise. And to function optimally, many muscles work together. For example, we target chest muscles when doing pushups. However, other muscles like the triceps and shoulders are often involved in the same exercise. When we target only one muscle, the supportive muscles can suffer neglect. The supporting muscles are used just as much as the "main" muscle. So, when we are trying to strengthen our chest muscles, other muscles are getting some work too.

Our bodies have over 600 muscles. Regarding strength training, most people target six to seven different muscle groups. They are:

- Shoulders
- Back
- Chest
- Arms
- Abs
- Hips
- Legs

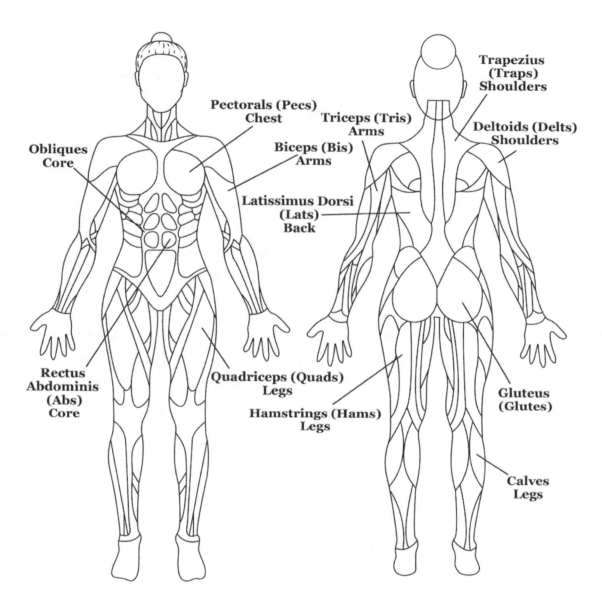

In my first book, Strength and Conditioning Training for Seniors Over 60, I compiled one of the most comprehensive lists of strength and conditioning (S&C) exercises in the market. The book focuses primarily on building more strength in the seven muscle groups listed above and is a "broad stroke" of the most beneficial exercises to increase general strength and muscle growth.

Contrastingly, this book dials into specific exercises that are related to the categories of balance, bones, and posture. While there are some balance-related exercises and workouts in my first book that will overlap here, this book is more of a detailed brushstroke.

How much time to put into each workout routine and why?

This is a common question. The problem with that question is that there is no simple, straightforward answer. The answer is that it depends. There is no single workout time that works perfectly for everybody. But we can at least find common ground regarding the issue of time.

When answering this question, there are a few things to consider:

Fitness levels

What's your overall fitness level? For a beginner, spending hours working out may come with more significant risks than rewards. You'll burn out, push your body too far too soon, or get injured. Beginners may want to start with shorter workouts, 20-30 minutes or less. Even if you can only muster 10 mins, do it.

My college wrestling coach used to say, "busy feet are happy feet," which translated to the more often you can keep your feet moving during a match, the better position you'll be in to win (and be happy). The same applies to us here and now. We just need to keep moving in the time we've allotted for our workouts, whether it's 10 minutes or 60.

As our strength and balance improve (along with our confidence), we can add more minutes to our workouts. According to the American Heart Association, the typical adult should perform at least 75-150 minutes of strength training and aerobic activity weekly. The same suggestions recommend at least three 40-minute workout sessions per week. If it's too much, then even 10-15 minutes will do. It's better to complete even a 10-minute workout than to not do anything. Remember, busy feet are happy feet.

Type of exercise

How strenuous is the exercise? The more intense a workout, the less time we should spend on it. So, for example, it's not impossible to maintain a 30-minute brisk walk on the treadmill but good luck maintaining a sprint on the treadmill for that long. Even if we want to spend more time exercising, we must think about the workouts carefully. Then, we can go for shorter, more high-intensity workouts on busy days and do longer, lower-intensity workouts when we have more time.

Rest

If you've been to the gym, you've probably seen some people who look like they are doing nothing but just standing and idling. However, you may not know that these people are actually resting between sets, and it's often good for us to do the same depending on the intensity of our workouts.

Some exercises, particularly when strength training with weights, need rest, recovery, and preparation. While some may do a 30-minute strength training session, only 20 minutes may involve the actual lifting. And then, add an additional 10 minutes to the workout session for stretching and recovery (with a lot of hydration).

Commitments

The most important question is, how much do we prioritize exercise, and how much time are we willing to put in? Our health should come first, and we should invest in it. I know family and career are important, and we may find ourselves cutting short an exercise routine to attend to other matters. That's okay.

As we know, even 10 minutes of workout is better than no workout. So be proud of whatever you have time for, no matter how the workout is.

The Exercises

In this chapter, the exercises will be listed per category (Balance, Bones, and Posture) and listed as either Beginner, Intermediate, or Advanced.

You'll see that each exercise has benefits beyond just general balance, bones, or posture, from toning muscles to building your core to helping relieve stress. And each one of them often benefits multiple muscle groups and joints.

Each exercise contains illustrations showing the mechanics of each movement. In addition, the text will outline the body part(s) involved, the "benefit" of the exercise, and a description of "how to" perform it. There are also videos you can reference, as noted below in the video section.

You will also see the recommended number of repetitions (reps) if you want to do these separately from a workout. In the workout chapter (Ch 9), these numbers of reps may change slightly since the workouts include doing several exercises together.

Balance Exercises

The exercises in this section will help increase your balance in specific areas. While there are 20 total balance exercises listed, there are many more than you see here. I've simply cherry-picked some of my favorites exclusively for this book, as I feel like these 20 truly maximize what we need to accomplish in creating improved balance.

Bones Exercises

While these are similar in scope to balance exercises and often accomplish similar objectives, this category of exercises is more specific to helping create better bone strength and fighting osteoporosis. Many of the balance and posture exercises in the book will also contribute to better bone strength. However, these 20 total exercises in this category are some of my favorites and are some of the best bone-strengthening exercises that I've picked for you.

Posture Exercises

These 20 exercises are more central to improving our posture than those in the previous two categories. But I'll say it again, many of these movements also overlap and will help improve balance and bones too. These 20 favorite cherry-picked exercises are just slightly more relevant to the application of creating better posture.

Warm-Up Exercises

I've included a few warm-up exercises, which will be listed at the end of this chapter, to roll into the Chapter 9 workouts. I picked some that are universal and easy to execute and apply. If you perform 1-2 minutes of each warmup exercise, that should be sufficient for these workouts. You should do 2-4 warmup exercises per workout. More of this is explained in Chapter 9.

All Exercises

I encourage you to try all these exercises to see which ones benefit you the most. Then, in addition to the individual workouts in Chapter 9, you can start crafting your own workouts based on your needs and goals. Think of the following exercises as items on a menu that you can select for your "workout meal," similar to a "pick 3" or an ala carte approach to dining. This is easier once you get to know the exercises and your body.

Consider keeping a chair handy for balance, especially during the balance exercises. This can offer you a safety net as you're becoming familiar with the exercises.

Lastly, before diving in, some of these exercises will feel foreign until you've worked on them for a bit. So please do not become discouraged if you can't perform them immediately. You will be able to over time, with practice.

Health Disclaimer

Your health and safety come first. To do any of the workouts mentioned in this book, you should be physically healthy with no medical complications or impairments that might impede your workout plans. I cannot give medical advice. My goal is to offer you the best exercises, workout programs, nutritional information, and how to best achieve the goals you set for yourself. My aim is not to advise you about your personal physical health or ability or to give you detailed nutritional plans for your specific body in this book. If you are not confident that you should begin exercising, please consult your doctor.

Video

All the exercises you see in this book can also be found in video form by scanning this QR code and tapping on the link the code reveals. This will bring you to a YouTube page that will contain the names and "how to" of each exercise.

WEB LINK FOR VIDEO EXERCISES

https://www.youtube.com/@SilverFoxesFitness/videos

QR CODE FOR VIDEO EXERCISES

20
BALANCE EXERCISES

Exercise: Flamingo | **Difficulty:** Beginner

Body Part: Core, Abs, Hips, Legs | **Benefit:** Helps hip joints for better mobility.

How To: Standing upright with the back of a chair, place your hands on the top of the chair to stabilize yourself. Next, slowly raise one foot with your knee pointing at the back of the chair. Hold this position for 5-10 seconds. Then, return your foot to the floor slowly and repeat the motion with the other leg. Do this 12-15 times.

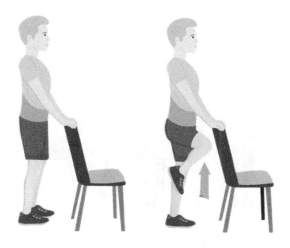

Exercise: Hip Circles | **Difficulty:** Beginner

Body Part: Hips, Low Back, Spine | **Benefit:** Stretches hips, helps with balance and spine.

How To: Standing straight with feet shoulder-width apart and eyes forward, place your hands on your hips. Slowly and gently start to rotate your hips around in a circle. Do this 5 times to one side, then gradually stop and reverse directions for 5 times.

Exercise: Lateral Stepping | **Difficulty:** Beginner

Body Part: Core: Hips, Legs | **Benefit:** Coordination and balance in small spaces.

How To: Standing straight with eyes forward and feet close together, grasp the top of a chair's back with one hand. Slowly step to the side opposite of the chair, then slowly step back to the original position. Repeat this 10 times, rotate around, and do the other leg 10 times.

Exercise: Overhead Side Stretches | **Difficulty:** Beginner

Body Part: Hips, Shoulders, Back | **Benefit:** Stretches shoulders and core, helps balance

How To: Standing straight with feet slightly more than shoulder-width apart and eyes forward, reach up to the ceiling with both arms. Place your palms together and slowly lean to the side, keeping your feet stationary. When you reach about 25 degrees, slowly come back up and repeat to the opposite side. Do this 5-10 times per side.

Exercise: Tightropes | **Difficulty:** Beginner

Body Part: Core, Abs, Hips, Legs | **Benefit:** Improves balance and coordination.

How To: Stand straight with one foot in front of the other. Place your hands on your hips or out to the side. Slowly put one foot directly in front of the other, with your heel just before your toes. Continue this motion as if walking straight on a tightrope. It may help to use a 6-foot piece of string or yarn as a marker to walk. Do this for 1-2 minutes.

Exercise: Weight Shifts | **Difficulty:** Beginner

Body Part: Legs, Ankles | **Benefit:** A great beginning balance and coordination exercise.

How To: Stand with feet shoulder-width apart, eyes looking forward. Make sure your feet are evenly distributing your weight. Keep your hands at your sides and move your weight to one side while picking up the opposite foot slightly off the ground. Hold the position for 15-20 seconds, then return the foot to the ground. Do this 5-7 times per side and consider increasing the time with each repetition.

Exercise: Balance Walking | **Level of Difficulty:** Intermediate

Body Part: Core, Abs, Hips, Shoulders, Legs | **Benefit:** Increases balance, ankle stabilization.

How To: With eyes forward and feet shoulder-width apart, bring your arms up so they are parallel to the floor. Slowly lift one leg, pointing your knee outward, and hold for 1-2 seconds. Next, slowly put your raised foot forward and down, walking exaggeratedly with a big step. The key is to hold your knee up for 1-2 seconds. Repeat this walking motion with the other foot. Do this for 30-60 seconds.

Exercise: Clock Reaches | **Level of Difficulty:** Intermediate

Body Part: Core, Shoulders, Hips, Legs | **Benefit:** Balance, coordination, and fixed standing.

How To: Standing straight with eyes forward and feet close together, grasp the top of a chair with one hand. Imagine you have a "clock's hands," and noon is directly in front of you, and 6 o'clock is directly behind you. Slowly raise your outer knee, and slowly raise your hand to the 3 o'clock position (to the side). Next, move your hand slowly to noon and then back to 3. Repeat this motion 5 times, then switch arms and legs.

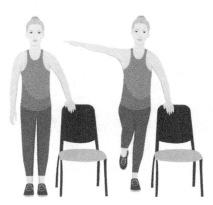

Exercise: Dead Bugs | **Difficulty:** Intermediate

Body Part: Core, Abs, Shoulders | **Benefit:** Strengthens core, helps coordination.

How To: Lying on your back, put your arms straight into the air and raise your legs so your knees are bent at 90 degrees. Slowly lower one leg so it's straight and just above the floor while lowering the opposite side arm to just above the floor. Slowly alternate the opposite leg and arm to the same positions. Do this 10-15 times.

Exercise: Grapevine | **Difficulty:** Intermediate

Body Part: Hips, Glutes, Ankles | **Benefit:** Coordination, stability to lower extremities.

How To: Standing upright with feet slightly more than shoulder-width apart, put your hands straight down at your side, looking forward. Your knees should not be locked but bent very slightly. Slowly cross your right leg in front of your left leg and hold the position for 2 seconds. Bring your right leg back to the original spot and do the same motion with your left leg. Do this 8-10 times for each leg. If needed, bring your arms up at your sides for additional stability.

Exercise: Mountain Climbers | **Difficulty:** Intermediate

Body Part: Shoulders, Abs, Legs, Glutes | **Benefit:** Coordination, cardiovascular health.

How To: Stand with feet shoulder-width apart, reach up with one arm (as if climbing), and bring up the opposite knee/leg to about 90 degrees. Return to the original position and promptly perform the same motion with the other arm and leg. Do this 10-15 times.

Exercise: Side Lunges | **Level of Difficulty:** Intermediate

Body Part: Legs (Quads, Hamstrings), Hips | **Benefit:** Strengthens legs, helps balance.

How To: Stand straight with feet slightly less than shoulder-width, and place your hands up to your chest. With eyes forward, slowly pick one leg up slightly and "lunge" this leg to the side. Bend at the knee, keep most of your weight on the bent knee side while keeping the other leg secure. Return to the starting position and repeat with the other leg. Do this 8-10 times per leg.

Exercise: One-Leg Stand | **Difficulty:** Intermediate

Body Part: Glutes, Ankles, Knees | **Benefit:** Balance and coordination, strengthens legs.

How To: Stand with feet slightly less than shoulder-width apart, hands at your sides, and eyes forward. Slowly bend at the right knee, keeping your left foot planted. Continue lifting your right foot up/back with the heel pointed up and toe pointed down until your leg reaches 45 degrees. Now balance on your left leg for 10 seconds. Bring your leg back down and alternate with your left leg. Do this 5-10 times per leg.

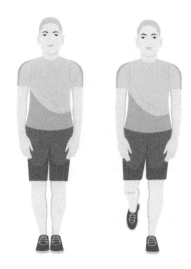

Exercise: Bird Dog | **Difficulty:** Advanced

Body Part: Back, Core, Shoulders | **Benefit:** Helps lower back injury, core.

How To: Start on your knees and hands, with hands just under your shoulders and knees, even with your hips. Slowly raise one arm and the opposite leg simultaneously, pointing both forward and backward, respectively. Hold for 2-3 seconds, then slowly return to the original position. Do this 10 times per side.

Exercise: Drinking Bird | **Difficulty:** Advanced

Body Part: Shoulders, Core, Glutes, Hips | **Benefit:** Multiple muscles, coordination.

How To: Standing straight with your feet hip-width apart, slowly bend one knee and bring your leg backward. Simultaneously raise both hands outward as you bend forward, keeping your weight on one leg. Slowly return to the original position and alternate legs. Do this 10 times.

Exercise: Fighter Squats | **Difficulty:** Advanced

Body Part: Glutes, Hips, Abs, Legs, Back | **Benefit:** Multiple muscles, cardiovascular.

How To: Placing your feet slightly more than shoulder-width apart, squat down until you're almost seated with your butt touching an imaginary chair. Return up and turn your torso to the right while throwing a left-hand punch. Come back down to the squat position and then do the same thing to the opposite side. Do this 12-15 times.

Exercise: Rock the Boat | **Difficulty:** Advanced

Body Part: Quadriceps, Hamstrings, Hips, Ankles | **Benefit:** Balance, stretching.

How To: Stand with feet shoulder-width apart and place your weight onto one foot to balance. Lift the knee of your other leg so that your foot is off the ground. Slowly extend the foot that is off the ground until you cannot stretch it out anymore. (You may not get fully extended depending on how flexible your hamstrings are). Hold this for 15-20 seconds. Bring the leg back down to the ground. Do this 8-10 times per leg.

Exercise: Squatting Reaches | **Difficulty:** Advanced

Body Part: Legs, Glutes, Shoulders | **Benefit:** Works multiple muscles, joints.

How To: Stand straight with feet shoulder-width apart and eyes forward. Slowly lower your butt to a 45-degree angle while raising your arms above your head. Hold the squat for 1-2 seconds, and slowly return to the original position. Do this 10-12 times.

Exercise: Standing Bird Dog | **Difficulty:** Advanced

Body Part: Hamstrings, Back, Ankles | **Benefit:** Coordination, stability, core strength

How To: Stand straight with your feet together, less than shoulder-width apart, arms at your side. Start leaning forward, looking down, while keeping the right leg planted, bringing your left leg straight back simultaneously. Keep your left arm at your side, and slowly bring your right arm up over your head. While keeping your back as flat as possible, slowly straighten your right (standing) leg.

Exercise: Tree Pose | **Difficulty:** Advanced

Body Part: Legs, Abs, Shoulders | **Benefit:** Balance, coordination, strengthens core.

How To: Stand straight with feet shoulder-width apart, eyes looking forward. Put the palms of your hands together in a prayer-like pose. Slowly shift weight to one foot (keeping it on the floor) and slowly move your other foot up past your knee. Place the bottom of your foot onto your inner thigh above your knee. Then slowly lift your palms upward, keeping them together until your hands are above your head. Hold this position for 10 seconds and breathe deeply.

20

BONE EXERCISES

Exercise: Back Extension | **Difficulty:** Beginner

Body Part: Back, Neck | **Benefit:** Helps stretch lower/mid back, strengthens the spine.

How To: Lying face down on a mat, keep your feet and legs together and arms at your side. Slowly raise your upper body (head, shoulders, and back) and hold that position for 10 seconds while pushing your arms to your sides. For a more challenging version, try raising both legs up slowly together simultaneously with your upper body and hold that position for 10 seconds. Do 8-10 of these.

Exercise: Clam Shell | **Difficulty:** Beginner

Body Part: Hips, Glutes, Legs | **Benefit:** Strengthens glutes and hips, stability.

How To: Lying on your side with knees bent and hips aligned, make sure that your feet and ankles are together. Keeping your feet together, lift your top knee as high as possible and hold this open for 8-10 seconds. Slowly bring your knee back down to the original position and take a deep breath. Do 10-15 of these on each side.

Exercise: Standing Hip Abduction | **Difficulty:** Beginner

Body Part: Hips | **Benefit:** Strengthens hips, low back, and helps balance.

How To: Standing straight with your eyes forward, grab the back top of a chair to steady yourself. Place your free hand on your hip and slowly move your outside leg away from your body while keeping it straight. Hold your leg out for 1-2 seconds and slowly return to the original position. Do this 8-10 times for each leg.

Exercise: Stair Step Ups | **Difficulty:** Beginner

Body Part: Legs (Quads), Glutes, Knees | **Benefit:** Stability, balance, and coordination.

How To: Stand near the stairs and place your inside hand on a railing or wall for balance. With one leg, slowly step up to the first stair and bring your other leg up, ensuring both feet are secure at the top. Slowly bring the second leg down to the floor and then the first leg. Do this 10-15 times.

Exercise: Wall Pushups | **Level of Difficulty:** Beginner

Body Part: Chest, Arms, Shoulders | **Benefit:** Strengthens pushing muscles.

How To: Feet shoulder-width apart, about 2-3 feet away from the wall. Slowly place your hands on the wall just below the shoulders. Keep your arms slightly bent, back straight, and eyes looking ahead at the wall. Slowly bend your elbows until your nose barely touches the wall. Then, slowly push back up to your original position. Do this 12-15 times. To change it up, try varying the width of your hands.

Exercise: Weighted Calf Raises | **Difficulty:** Beginner

Body Part: Legs (Calves), Glutes, Ankles | **Benefit:** Helps balance and coordination.

How To: Take light dumbbells in both hands, stand straight with feet hip-width apart and eyes forward. Slowly raise up on both feet's toes until you can't go any higher. Hold for 1-2 seconds and slowly return to the original position. Do this 10-12 times. You can also do this without weights, using a chair for balance.

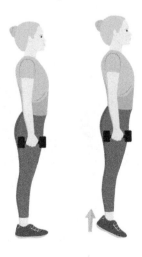

Exercise: Car Drivers | **Difficulty:** Intermediate

Body Part: Shoulders, Upper Back, Neck | **Benefit:** Shoulder, neck strength, and toning.

How To: This can be done with a book or any flat 1-2 pound object. With feet shoulder-width apart, head forward, and arms parallel to the ground, place your hands at 3 and 9 o'clock. Move the object away from you with arms fully extended. Rotate the object to the right to about 12 o'clock and then back to the left, again at 12 o'clock. Do this 8-12 times.

Exercise: Front Shoulder Raises | **Difficulty:** Intermediate

Body Part: Shoulders, Back | **Benefit:** Strengthens and tones shoulders and upper back.

How To: Using light dumbbells, water bottles, or nothing at all, stand straight up with your shoulders slightly back and a slight arch in your back. Slowly raise one arm just past parallel to the ground and then back down. Alternate with the other arm using the same motion. Do this 12-15 times for each arm. Be careful not to rock or use your body weight to force the weight up, using only your shoulders to bring up the weight.

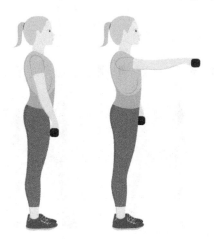

Exercise: Lying Dumbbell Chest Press | **Difficulty:** Intermediate

Body Part: Chest, Shoulders, Triceps | **Benefit:** Strengthens and tones chest, shoulders, arms.

How To: Take light dumbbells in each hand and lie down with your back on the floor and your knees bent. Position the dumbbells at chest height, and before you press the weight up, inhale to fill your lungs. Then, press up and exhale until your arms are fully extended. As you bring the weights back down, inhale again until your arms return to where you started. Do this 12-15 times. This is a good exercise do to on a weight bench.

Exercise: Overhead Shoulder Press | **Difficulty:** Intermediate

Body Part: Shoulders, Upper Back | **Benefit:** Strengthens and tones shoulders, upper back.

How To: With your head forward and hands holding small weights, start with elbows bent just past 90 degrees and palms facing outward. Slowly press the weight up until your arms are fully extended, and then slowly come back down and repeat. Try to keep your back from arching too much, as the lift should come from your shoulders. Aim for 12-15 reps. You can also do this same exercise with palms facing inward or backward for variety.

Exercise: Pushups | **Difficulty:** Intermediate

Body Part: Chest, Triceps, Shoulders | **Benefit:** Strengthens upper body, bones, joints.

How To: Start by lying on the floor, belly down, with your hands slightly more shoulder-width apart. Put your palms flat on the floor and raise your heels towards your butt until your legs are about 90 degrees. Slowly press your palms down into the floor, pushing your body up while your knees stay on the floor. Push up until your arms are fully extended, while keeping your back straight.

Exercise: Side Shoulder Raises | **Difficulty:** Intermediate

Body Part: Shoulders, Neck | **Benefit:** Strengthens/tones shoulders and upper back.

How To: Like Front Shoulder Raises, you can use a light weight or no weight. Form is more important than how much you lift. With your arms at your sides, slowly lift your hands/weights to just past parallel to the ground. Be sure to breathe in when lifting and out when coming down. 12-15 times is a good goal. Keep your body straight without rocking.

Exercise: Standing Bicep Curls | **Difficulty:** Intermediate

Body Part: Arms, Shoulder, Upper Back, Wrist | **Benefit:** Pulling and grip strength.

How To: Stand with knees slightly bent, eyes looking forward. With a light dumbbell in each arm, in front of your thighs, bring one arm up slowly towards your shoulder in a curl-like motion. Keep your elbows close to your body. Briefly stop at the top, then slowly return to the original position. Do the same with the other arm, being careful not to rock back and forth. Do this 12-15 times per arm.

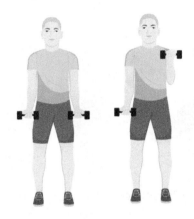

Exercise: Upright Rows | **Difficulty:** Intermediate

Body Part: Upper Back, Shoulders | **Benefit:** Strengthens/tones upper back and shoulders.

How To: Stand with feet shoulder-width apart, keep eyes forward and arms resting on your thighs, with or without light dumbbells. Holding weights/hands close to your body, slowly bring your elbows up to where they're pointing straight out from your body, even with your shoulders. You should feel your shoulder blades come together. Pause briefly and come back down slowly to the original position. Do this 10-15 times.

Exercise: Bear Crawl | **Difficulty:** Advanced

Body Part: Core, Glutes, Hips, Shoulders, Wrists | **Benefit:** Multiple muscle groups, joints.

How To: Starting on your hands and knees, with your back flat and hands and legs at 90 degrees to the floor, slowly lift your knees a few inches from the ground. Begin crawling with one hand moving forward and the opposite leg moving forward simultaneously. Crawl in this position for 15-30 seconds, both forward and backward.

Exercise: Bent Over Rows | **Difficulty:** Advanced

Body Part: Upper Back, Shoulders, Arms | **Benefit:** Improves spinal stability.

How To: Using a chair, place one hand on its top and hold a small (or no) weight. Bend the knees and hips to about 45 degrees. Pull the weight up slowly until it reaches your stomach, returning it in the same fashion. The key is ensuring your back stays straight or slightly arched but not hunched over. Do these 10-12 times per arm.

Exercise: Bent Shoulder Raises | **Difficulty:** Advanced

Body Part: Shoulders, Back | **Benefit:** Strengthens shoulders, joints, and tendons.

How To: While holding small dumbbells in each hand with the dumbbells together, stand with your feet shoulder-width apart. Bending slightly at the knees and forward at the waist (about 40 degrees) while keeping your back flat. Bend at the elbows slightly, and lift both arms outward to the side (while inhaling) until they are almost parallel with the floor. Slowly lower the dumbbells back together (while exhaling) and pause for 1 second. Do this 12-15 times. You can also try this seated on a bench or chair.

Exercise: Lunging Bicep Curl | **Difficulty:** Advanced

Body Part: Biceps, Legs, Glutes | **Benefit:** Works multiple muscles, helps balance.

How To: Take light dumbbells (or no weight) in both hands, stand straight with your legs together and your eyes forward. Simultaneously and slowly lunge one leg forward while bringing up both hands and weights in a curl motion towards your chest. Then, slowly return both your arms and first leg to the original position. Do this 10-12 times.

Exercise: Triceps Kickbacks | **Difficulty:** Advanced

Body Part: Arms, Upper Back | **Benefit:** Strengthens and tones the triceps muscles.

How To: Take a light dumbbell in each hand and stand with feet shoulder-width apart. Bend at your waist to about a 45-degree angle. Bring the weights close to your body, bending at the elbows at another 45-degree angle. While keeping your elbows still, slowly take your hands (and weights) back behind you until your arms are fully extended. Make sure to stay in your original bent-over position. Then, slowly bring your weights back to the original spot. Do this 12-15 times. Try it without weights if it's too heavy at first.

Exercise: Wall Sits | **Difficulty:** Advanced

Body Part: Legs, Knees, Core, Ankles | **Benefit:** Leg and core strength, balance.

How To: Stand with feet shoulder-width apart, back facing the wall about 2 feet away. Lean back on the wall and slide down to about a 60-75 degree angle. Stop for 1-2 seconds to test your strength. If able, move down to 90 degrees and hold for a count of 10. Come back up and do this 8-10 times. Use your hands on the wall to move back up to starting position.

20

POSTURE EXERCISES

Exercise: Bicep Stretches | **Difficulty:** Beginner

Body Part: Bicep, Shoulders | **Benefit:** Stretches arms, shoulders, and spine.

How To: Sitting on the floor with knees bent, slowly lean back, and place your hands flat behind you. Very slowly, scoot your butt forward until you feel a slight stretch in your arms. Breathe in/out deeply and hold for about 10 seconds, then return to the original position. Do this 8-10 times.

Exercise: Chest Openers | **Difficulty:** Beginner

Body Part: Chest, Shoulders, Back | **Benefit:** Stretches upper body, releases tension.

How To: Standing or kneeling, in your best posture possible, place both hands behind your head, eyes forward. Point your elbows outward, away from your body. Take a deep breath and gently push your chest out and arch your back while keeping your hands on your head. Next, slowly exhale and bring your elbows together slowly while curving your back. Bringing your head down slightly until you feel a slight stretch in your upper back. Do this 8-10 times.

Exercise: Child's Pose | **Difficulty:** Beginner

Body Part: Shoulders, Back, Legs | **Benefit:** Helps stretch and relax multiple muscles.

How To: Starting with both knees on the floor and sitting back on your hunches, slowly bring your face towards the floor and lean forward, bringing your hands up above your head. Place your hands on the floor and extend them away slowly from your body. When you feel a mild stretch in your shoulders, hold for 5 seconds, then release the stretch. Do this 8-10 times.

Exercise: Hip Hinges | **Difficulty:** Beginner

Body Part: Hips, Abs, Core | **Benefit:** Strengthens and creates flexibility in hips.

How To: Standing straight with eyes forward and feet hip-width apart, place your hands on your hips. Slowly hinge forward from the hips, keeping your legs and back straight, and bend to about 45-90 degrees. Then, slowly return to the original position. Do this 10-12 times.

Exercise: Neck Stretches | **Difficulty:** Beginner

Body Part: Neck, Upper Spine | **Benefit:** Stretches and warms up neck muscles.

How To (Side): Make sure your torso and head are straight, eyes looking forward. Slowly bend your head to one side while pulling gently with your hand on that same side. Hold for 15-20 seconds and slowly return your head to an upright position. Do this 5-7 times per side.

How To (Front): Make sure your torso and head are straight, eyes looking forward. Slowly bend your head down and place your hands behind your head. Very gently, pull down on your head, tucking your chin until you feel a mild stretch in your neck. Hold for 15-20 seconds, and slowly move your head back to its original position. Do this 5-7 times taking deep breaths during reps.

Exercise: One Arm Hugs | **Difficulty:** Beginner

Body Part: Shoulders, Back, Chest | **Benefit:** Stretches multiple upper body muscles.

How To: Sitting on the floor with your legs crossed, shoulders square, and eyes forward, bring one arm across your chest above your shoulder. With your other arm, gently pull your upper arm back (above the elbow) until you feel mild tension in your upper arm. Hold this for 10 seconds, then change arms. Do this 5 times per arm.

Exercise: Shoulder Pull Back | **Difficulty:** Beginner

Body Part: Shoulders, Upper Back | **Benefit:** Reduces tension in shoulders and back.

How To: Standing straight with shoulders square, feet together, and eyes forward, slowly inhale deeply and bring your shoulders backward while slowly pushing out your chest. Hold this for 3-5 seconds. Exhale and return to the original position. Do this 8-10 times.

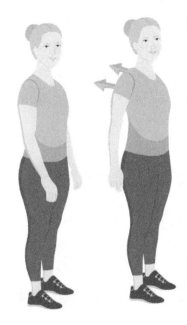

Exercise: Abdominal Bridges | **Difficulty:** Intermediate

Body Part: Core, Abs, Back, Pelvis | **Benefit:** Strengthens core muscles and lower back.

How To: Lying on the floor, rest on your elbows with your hands below your face and pelvis down. Slowly raise your hips, keeping your knees on the floor. Hold in the up position for 1-2 seconds, tighten your abs, then slowly come back down to the floor. Do this 10-12 times.

Exercise: Back Flexor Stretch | **Difficulty:** Intermediate

Body Part: Back, Shoulders, Core | **Benefit:** Stretches back, shoulders, and tones abs.

How To: Lay flat on the floor with your feet flat and knees pointed up to the sky. Place your hands above your head in a resting position. Slowly bring your knees toward your head while simultaneously reaching your hands to your calves (below your shins). Breathe deeply and hold your position for 5 seconds, feeling the pull in your back and shoulders. Slowly return to the starting position. Do this 8-10 times.

Exercise: Cat-Cow Stretch | **Difficulty:** Intermediate

Body Part: Back, Neck, Core | **Benefit:** Stretches neck, core, spine, helps with breathing.

How To: Start with both knees and hands on the floor, place your knees hip-width apart and your hands shoulder-width apart. Slowly arch your back into a scared cat-like position while relaxing your head downward. Hold for 2-3 seconds and slowly return to the cow-like position. Bring your head up with your eyes forward and back arched. Do this 8-10 times.

Exercise: Glute Bridge | **Difficulty:** Intermediate

Body Part: Core, Abs, Glutes | **Benefit:** Strengthens core, lower back, and butt.

How To: Lying on your back, bend your knees, and keep your heels under your knees and arms at your side. Slowly raise your pelvis until your thighs align with your upper body. On the way up, squeeze your glutes (butt) and abs. Hold at the top for 5-10 seconds. Then, slowly return to the original position. Do this 10 times.

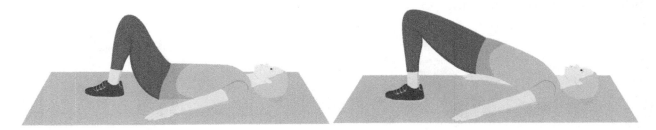

Exercise: Glute Stretch | **Difficulty:** Intermediate

Body Part: Glutes, Hips | **Benefit:** Stretches glutes and helps hip flexibility.

How To: Sitting upright on a chair, place both feet flat on the floor and then cross one leg over the opposite knee. Grasp your knee with both hands and slowly pull it forward towards your shoulder while leaning slightly forward towards your knee for 5-10 seconds. Do this 5-7 times per leg.

Exercise: Kneeling Hip Flexor | **Difficulty:** Intermediate

Body Part: Hips, Legs, Lower Back | **Benefit:** Stretches hips, quads, helps posture.

How To: Putting one knee on the floor with your toes tucked and the other knee forward with your foot flat, make a 90-degree angle with your forward leg. Simultaneously place both hands (one on top of the other) on your extended knee for balance. Keep your torso upright while slowly leaning forward until you feel a slight stretch in your forward leg. Hold for 20-30 seconds, then alternate legs.

Exercise: Knee-to-Chest Stretch | **Difficulty:** Intermediate

Body Part: Back, Abs, Back | **Benefit:** Stretches lower back, tones abs, helps spine.

How To: Lying flat on your back, place your feet flat on the floor while bending your knees. Slowly bring one knee up until you can hold it just below the knee with your hand. Then bring the second knee up and hold it with your other hand. Gently bring your hands together and lace your fingers, locking your knees into your chest. If you have back issues, do not lock your fingers, and simply hold your knees with your hands. Hold this position for about 5 seconds. Do this stretch 8-10 times.

Exercise: Wall Angels | **Difficulty:** Intermediate

Body Part: Shoulders, Upper Back | **Benefit:** Strengthens spine, helps posture.

How To: With your back against a wall, put your hands up and bend your arms to 90 degrees. Keeping feet shoulder-width apart, slowly reach toward the ceiling keeping your arms and shoulder blades flat against the wall. Come back down in the same slow motion making sure your arms and blades stay against the wall. Do this 10-12 times.

Exercise: Downward Dog | **Difficulty:** Advanced

Body Part: Legs, Calves, Spine, Shoulders | **Benefit:** Relieves stress and mild back pain.

How To: Starting with both hands and knees on the floor, place your hands (with your fingers spread) under your shoulders, knees under your hips, and maintain a flat back. Push your feet back, placing them flat onto the floor while simultaneously straightening knees and brining hips up while slowly straightening your legs and arms. When fully stretched, your body should resemble an inverted V, with your head relaxed. Breathe deeply for 30 seconds and feel the stretch in multiple areas of your body.

Exercise: Pigeon Pose | **Difficulty:** Advanced

Body Part: Shoulders, Neck, Back, Hips | **Benefit:** Opens hips, strengthens spine.

How To: Starting on hands and knees, slowly bring one leg up and underneath your hips and slowly scoot the other leg backward until you feel a stretch in your glutes. Bring your torso forward and extend your hands so they're flat. Rest here for 10-15 seconds, then slowly raise your head up and look at the sky. Use your arms and fingers as support. Hold for 10-15 seconds. Do each leg 5-7 times.

Exercise: Plank (Standard, Forearm) | **Difficulty:** Advanced

Body Part: Core, Glutes, Shoulders | **Benefit:** Strengthens core, prevents mild back pain.

How To: Starting on hands and knees, place your hands (with your fingers spread) under your shoulders, knees under your hips, and maintain a flat back. While keeping your arms static, slowly walk your feet back until your legs are completely straight with your toes tucked. Breathe deeply for 20-30 seconds while feeling the effects of the stretch in your core, glutes, and shoulders. To vary the exercise, move down to your forearms and hold for 20-30 seconds.

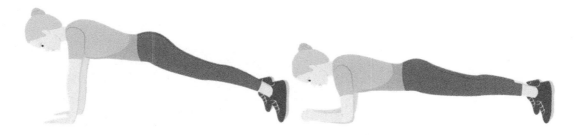

Exercise: Warrior I | **Difficulty:** Advanced

Body Part: Back, legs, shoulders | **Benefit:** Balance, posture, stability.

How To: Standing straight with feet slightly less than shoulder-width apart, move one leg backward until it's fully extended. Your forward, non-extended leg should end up slightly past your chest. Maintain balance with your arms at your side, then slowly raise your arms above your head to the sky and look straight ahead. Place your back heel down to the floor so your foot is flat and arch your lower back slightly. Breathe deeply and hold that position for 10-15 seconds. Do each leg 5 times.

Exercise: Warrior II and Warrior III | **Difficulty:** Advanced

Body Part: Back, legs, shoulders | **Benefit:** Balance, posture, stability.

How To: (Warrior II): While in Warrior I pose, shift your back foot so your toes are pointed out, almost perpendicular to your extended leg. Slowly point your arm (palm down) on the same side as your forward leg straight out in front. Slowly take your other arm (palm down) back to align with your back leg. Both arms and hands should be parallel to the floor.

How To: (Warrior III): While in Warrior II pose, slowly bring your back arm up and even to your forward arm. Push your balance forward to rest on the lead leg while bringing your back leg off the floor. Point your back leg straight behind you, parallel to the floor. Maintain balance on one leg, with both arms forward (palms together) and parallel to the floor.

Warrior I

Warrior II

Warrior III

4

WARM-UP EXERCISES

Exercise: Jumping Jacks

Body Part: Shoulders, Legs, Hips, Knees, Ankles | **Benefit:** Warm-up, balance, stability.

How To: Standing with feet together and arms at your sides, look straight ahead with your body straight except for a slight bend in your knees. Jump your feet out to the side (just past shoulder-width) while simultaneously bringing your arms up and over your head. Right after you land, jump back to your starting position. Do this 12-15 times.

Exercise: Marching in Place

Body Part: Legs, Arms | **Benefit:** Good warm-up for strength exercises, helps balance.

How To: Standing straight with shoulders square, feet together, and eyes forward, slowly begin marching. Exaggerate your arms and legs so your hands come as high as your face and knees to 45 degrees. Pick up the tempo slightly as you march but stay balanced. Focus on good breathing and form. Do this for 30 seconds.

Exercise: Sideways Shuffle

Body Part: Legs | **Benefit:** Good warm-up for strength exercises, helps balance and stability.

How To: Standing straight with feet slightly greater than shoulder-width apart, knees bent slightly, and eyes forward, slowly shuffle to one side. To "shuffle," bring one foot next to the other, never crossing your feet. If you have enough space, do this 3-4 times to the right and 3-4 times to the left. Keep going back and forth for 30 seconds.

Exercise: Arm Circles

Body Part: Shoulders, Neck | **Benefit:** A good warm-up for upper body exercises.

How To: Stand straight with feet shoulder-width apart, knees together, arms at your side, and eyes forward. Slowly lift your arms until they're parallel to the floor. Slow start circling your arms forward. Do this for 30 seconds. For variety, you can reverse direction and make the circles larger or smaller.

9

THE 15+ WORKOUTS

"A lot of people are afraid of heights. Not me, I'm afraid of widths."
– Steven Wright

———

This chapter contains fifteen unique workout routines specifically designed to aid in the improvement of our balance, bones, and posture. Each workout has a distinct purpose. The first nine are graded based on three levels of difficulty: Beginner, Intermediate, and Advanced.

There is one workout per level in each category. For example, there are three total beginner workouts: one in balance, one in bones, and one in posture. The same applies to the intermediate and advanced levels.

After the various levels of workouts, we have "combo" workouts that will combine two of the three categories. And lastly, we have three "hybrid" workouts that feature all three categories together. These are also graded as either Beginner, Intermediate, or Advanced.

Beyond those, there are infinite ways to "mix and match" exercises based on your specific needs. Hence the title "15+ Workouts". For example, if you want to focus more on lower back exercises, you can go back to Chapter 8 and cherry-pick those exercises to create an "ala carte" menu of exercises.

Remember, many of these exercises overlap. Some of the balance exercises are great for posture, and many of the bone exercises are great for balance, etc. Once you work your way through the exercises, you should be able to determine which ones are best for you. I'd encourage you to make notes of which ones you like the best so you can eventually apply them to create your own workouts. Remember, a PDF of just the exercises and workouts is included in the bonus section at the beginning of the book. You can print this and use it to easily follow along and make notes.

THE WORKOUTS

Here is a list of the fifteen workouts:

1. Balance Beginner
2. Balance Intermediate
3. Balance Advanced
4. Bones Beginner
5. Bones Intermediate
6. Bones Advanced
7. Posture Beginner
8. Posture Intermediate
9. Posture Advanced
10. Balance and Bones Combo
11. Balance and Posture Combo
12. Bones and Posture Combo
13. Balance, Bones, and Posture (Beginner)
14. Balance, Bones, and Posture (Intermediate)
15. Balance, Bones, and Posture (Advanced)

Note: For a detailed "how to" of each exercise, please refer to Chapter 8.

Workout Durations

Each workout is anywhere between 12-20 minutes in length. The Beginner workouts are shorter as they consist of five exercises, and the Intermediate and Advanced contain six.

All the exercises in the workouts (except for the warmups) are listed at 2 minutes per exercise. This is just a baseline. If you want to go longer or shorter, especially when starting out, please do so. This book is meant to help you get familiar enough with exercising that you start to develop a sense of what works best for your needs.

Form

We've already discussed this extensively in previous chapters, but I cannot stress it enough. Please remember that good form and breathing are essential when exercising. Be even more conscious of it as you near the end of your workouts, as that is when bad form starts to creep in when you're tired. Another essential tip going into the actual workouts is to stay hydrated. So, keep a water bottle nearby and take some swigs when you start to feel thirsty.

Warm-Ups: Pre-Workout

Warming up is an integral part of your pre-workout routine. The goal is to get your heart rate up and blood flowing faster than your resting levels. Even simple chores around the house will suffice. And remember, "busy feet are happy feet." Just be mindful that we don't want to be too tired at the warm-up stage. We just want to start getting our minds and bodies prepped for the next step…the workout.

For a detailed "how to" of each warmup exercise, please refer to Chapter 8. There are four warmup exercises to choose from in that chapter. Each workout in this chapter will describe the number of recommended warmups. Please choose your favorites.

Reminder

A PDF of just the exercises and workouts is included in the bonus section at the beginning of this book. You can print this and use it to easily follow along and make notes. There is also video examples of all exercises and workouts by scanning this QR code with your phone.

WEB LINK FOR VIDEO EXERCISES

https://www.youtube.com/@SilverFoxesFitness/videos

QR CODE FOR VIDEO EXERCISES

#1: BALANCE BEGINNER

Total workout time: About 12-15 mins | **Warmups:** Pick 2-3 warmups. See Ch. 8

1. The Flamingo (2 mins)
2. Hip Circles (2 mins)
3. Lateral Stepping (2 mins)
4. Overhead Side Stretch (2 mins)
5. Weight Shifts (2 mins)

QR Code for Workout Videos

Scan the QR code below to find video examples of all the exercises and workouts in this book, and more!

#2: BALANCE INTERMEDIATE

Total workout time: About 15-20 mins | **Warmups:** Pick 3 warmups. See Ch. 8

1. Balance Walking (2 mins)
2. Clock Reaches (2 mins)
3. Mountain Climbers (2 mins)
4. Side Lunges (2 mins)
5. Deadbugs (2 mins)
6. Grapevine (2 mins)

#3: BALANCE ADVANCED

Total workout time: About 15-20 mins | **Warmups:** Pick 3 warmups. See Ch. 8

1. Fighter Squats (2 mins)
2. Rock the Boat (2 mins)
3. Squatting Reaches (2 mins)
4. Tree Pose (2 mins)
5. Standing Bird Dog (2 mins)
6. Drinking Bird (2 mins)

#4: BONE BEGINNER

Total workout time: About 12-15 mins | **Warmups:** Pick 2-3 warmups. See Ch. 8

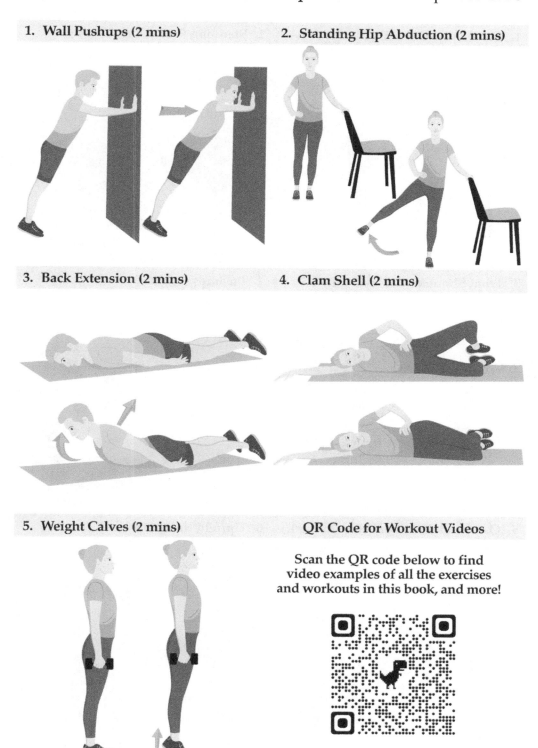

1. **Wall Pushups (2 mins)**

2. **Standing Hip Abduction (2 mins)**

3. **Back Extension (2 mins)**

4. **Clam Shell (2 mins)**

5. **Weight Calves (2 mins)**

QR Code for Workout Videos

Scan the QR code below to find video examples of all the exercises and workouts in this book, and more!

#5: BONE INTERMEDIATE

Total workout time: About 15-20 mins | **Warmups:** Pick 3 warmups. See Ch. 8

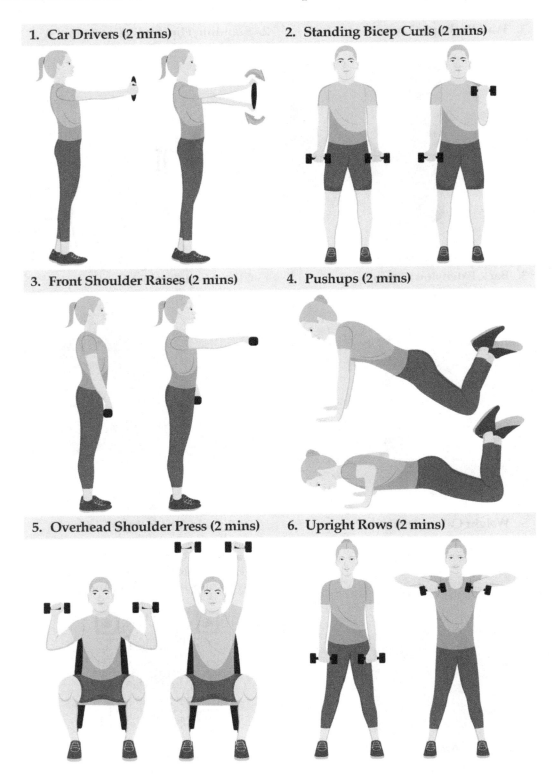

1. Car Drivers (2 mins)
2. Standing Bicep Curls (2 mins)
3. Front Shoulder Raises (2 mins)
4. Pushups (2 mins)
5. Overhead Shoulder Press (2 mins)
6. Upright Rows (2 mins)

#6: BONE ADVANCED

Total workout time: About 15-20 mins | **Warmups:** Pick 3 warmups. See Ch. 8

1. Bear Crawl (2 mins)

2. Tricep Kickbacks (2 mins)

3. Bent Over Rows (2 mins)

4. Bent Shoulder Raises (2 mins)

5. Lunging Bicep Curl (2 mins)

6. Wall Sits (2 mins)

#7: POSTURE BEGINNER

Total workout time: About 12-15 mins | **Warmups:** Pick 2-3 warmups. See Ch. 8

1. Neck Stretches (2 mins)
2. Shoulder Pull Back (2 mins)
3. Hip Hinges (2 mins)
4. Chest Openers (2 mins)
5. One Arm Hugs (2 mins)

QR Code for Workout Videos

Scan the QR code below to find video examples of all the exercises and workouts in this book, and more!

#8: POSTURE INTERMEDIATE

Total workout time: About 15-20 mins | **Warmups:** Pick 3 warmups. See Ch. 8

1. Abdominal Bridges (2 mins)
2. Cat Cow Stretch (2 mins)
3. Back Flexor Stretch (2 mins)
4. Glute Stretch (2 mins)
5. Kneeling Hip Flexor (2 mins)
6. Wall Angels (2 mins)

#9: POSTURE ADVANCED

Total workout time: About 15-20 mins | **Warmups:** Pick 3 warmups. See Ch. 8

1. Plank (2 mins)
2. Pigeon Pose (2 mins)
3. Downward Dog (2 mins)
4. Warrior I (2 mins)
5. Warrior II (2 mins)
6. Warrior III (2 mins)

#10: BALANCE AND BONES COMBO

Total workout time: About 15-20 mins | **Warmups:** Pick 3 warmups. See Ch. 8

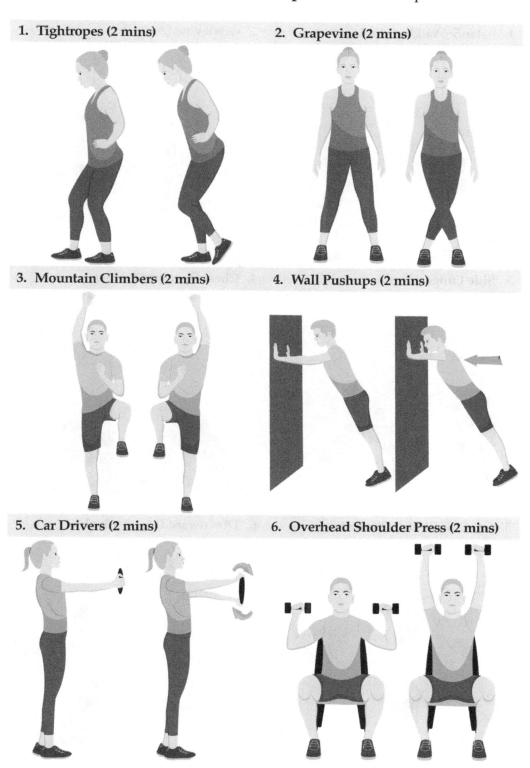

1. Tightropes (2 mins)
2. Grapevine (2 mins)
3. Mountain Climbers (2 mins)
4. Wall Pushups (2 mins)
5. Car Drivers (2 mins)
6. Overhead Shoulder Press (2 mins)

#11: BALANCE AND POSTURE COMBO

Total workout time: About 15-20 mins | **Warmups:** Pick 3 warmups. See Ch. 8

1. Balance Walking (2 mins)
2. Grapevine (2 mins)
3. Side Lunges (2 mins)
4. Chest Openers (2 mins)
5. Cat Cow Stretch (2 mins)
6. Downward Dog (2 mins)

#12: BONES AND POSTURE COMBO

Total workout time: About 15-20 mins | **Warmups:** Pick 3 warmups. See Ch. 8

1. Clam Shell (2 mins)
2. Front Shoulder Raises (2 mins)
3. Lying DB Chest Press (2 mins)
4. Child's Pose (2 mins)
5. One Arm Hugs (2 mins)
6. Back Flexor Stretch (2 mins)

#13: BALANCE, BONES, AND POSTURE HYBRID - BEGINNER

Total workout time: About 12-15 mins | **Warmups:** Pick 2-3 warmups. See Ch. 8

1. Weight Shifts (2 mins)
2. Lateral Stepping (2 mins)
3. Wall Pushups (2 mins)
4. Shoulder Pull Back (2 mins)
5. One Arm Hugs (2 mins)

QR Code for Workout Videos

Scan the QR code below to find video examples of all the exercises and workouts in this book, and more!

#14: BALANCE, BONES, AND POSTURE – INTERMEDIATE

Total workout time: About 15-20 mins | **Warmups:** Pick 3 warmups. See Ch. 8

1. Grapevine (2 mins)
2. Side Lunges (2 mins)
3. Upright Rows (2 mins)
4. Pushups (2 mins)
5. Cat Cow Stretch (2 mins)
6. Kneeling Hip Flexor (2 mins)

#15: BALANCE, BONES, AND POSTURE – ADVANCED

Total workout time: About 15-20 mins | **Warmups:** Pick 3 warmups. See Ch. 8

1. Fighter Squat (2 mins)
2. Tree Pose (2 mins)
3. Bent Over Rows (2 mins)
4. Lunging Bicep (2 mins)
5. Plank (2 mins)
6. Pigeon Pose (2 mins)

CONCLUSION

Believe it or not, by simply picking up this book, you took a significant step in acknowledging the need for a positive solution to improve your health. Recognizing this and taking action is huge step. So please realize the significance of this achievement.

As we've discussed, aging is a universal process that affects everyone. No one is exempt. However, this does not mean we should resign ourselves to the negative consequences of aging. Studies upon studies, as well as real-world testimonials, support this.

Taking proactive measures to maintain balance, better bones, and posture can distance us from injury. Falling and fractures, a common and often debilitating occurrence among seniors, can absolutely be prevented through balance, bones, and posture-related exercises. It's a fact.

Beyond fracture prevention, engaging in regular balance training offers numerous other benefits. Such as enhancing muscle tone, strengthening our hearts and blood flow, boosting cognitive ability, and improving reaction time. These advantages contribute to our overall well-being, significantly improve our quality of life, and may very well give us extra years.

While it may be tempting to ignore the rigors of exercise, it is critical to weigh the risks of living a sedentary lifestyle. On the flip side of the benefits, loss of bone density, muscle mass, increased frailty, higher risks of falls and injuries, diminished cognitive ability, and an elevated risk for chronic diseases are some of the potential consequences.

Beyond exercise, if there is only one change you have the bandwidth to make right now, then work on your diet. I know this may sound strange coming from a fitness book, but the fact is our bodies need good nutrition even above exercise. If the right fuel isn't getting into our bodies, we will suffer, regardless of exercise.

Eating the right foods and hydrating properly has immense benefits. It improves our energy, fights certain conditions, such as heart conditions, hypertension, improves sleep, and helps to repair and strengthen our muscles and bones.

As mentioned earlier in Chapter 6, some top nutrients we need as we age include:

- Calcium: Does more than just reinforce our bones. You can get plenty of calcium from dairy products, leafy greens, fish, beans, nuts, and seeds.
- Vitamin D: Being in the sunlight clears your head and strengthens your bones. Taking supplements also helps.
- Magnesium: Improves calcium absorption and can be found in spinach, seeds, beans, quinoa, and nuts.
- Water: The foundation of life. Sometimes, all you need to feel better is a glass of water.

By prioritizing good nutrition, physical activity (busy feet are happy feet), including exercise, we can significantly mitigate the adverse effects of aging and enjoy a healthier, more fulfilling life for ourselves and our loved ones. The benefits far outweigh any perceived barriers or challenges. So, embrace the opportunity "right now" to take control of your well-being to age gracefully. Unleash your "inner grapes" and create that fine wine that you will become.

By reading through these pages, you have already taken a huge step forward toward creating that fine wine. Your understanding of balance, bones, and posture has grown substantially, and now you have practical and strategic ways to start applying this knowledge. Well done!

Now, while this book covers a lot of ground, the human body is incredibly complex, and we'd need several encyclopedia-sized books to explore every single topic related to aging. Even as you read this book, many more studies on aging are being conducted, so I encourage you to continue your learning by exploring online resources, articles, blogs, and more books. As you learn and apply this knowledge, you'll find it's super fun to be healthy!

Of course, I will do my part and strive to deliver the best information on fitness for seniors. For this reason, please consider joining our email list and Facebook group (Give Me Strength - Fitness for Seniors) to receive the latest updates, including valuable nutrition advice, new exercises and techniques, and tips on goal setting and motivation.

Thank you for embarking on this journey with me through these pages. I hope you enjoyed it and will continue to learn and apply the knowledge you've gained. If you feel that you've benefitted from the book, please take a moment to recommend it to others and/or leave a brief review on Amazon.

Thanks very much. ~ Matthew

LEAVE A QUICK REVIEW, PAY IT FOWARD

I would be incredibly grateful if you would please take 30 seconds to write a brief review on Amazon, even if it's just a few sentences. Doing this "pays it forward" and lets others know you've benefited from the book, empowering them to achieve their health and fitness goals. Thank you.

Visit this webpage to leave a quick Amazon review: www.givemestrengthfitness.com/review2 or **scan this QR code**:

JOIN OUR COMMUNITY

Join our Facebook group! Just visit this webpage or scan the QR code below!
http://www.facebook.com/groups/givemestrength

Join our Instagram page! Just visit this website or scan the QR code below!

https://www.instagram.com/givemestrengthfitness

BIBLIOGRAPHY

Introduction

- Biostrap. (2022, March 4). Why Balance And Flexibility Training Are Essential To Balanced Fitness - Part 2 | Biostrap. *Biostrap*. Retrieved March 26, 2023, from https://biostrap.com/academy/why-balance-and-flexibility-training-are-essential-to-balanced-fitness-part-2/

- *Celebrities with Osteoporosis - London Osteoporosis Clinic.* (2021, April 24). London Osteoporosis Clinic. Retrieved March 26, 2023, from https://www.londonosteoporosisclinic.com/celebrities-with-osteoporosis/

- Ellis, L. (2022). What happens when old people don't exercise? *Hours for Seniors*. Retrieved March 26, 2023, from https://hoursforseniors.com/what-happens-when-old-people-dont-exercise/

- *Hip Fractures Among Older Adults | Fall Prevention | Injury Center | CDC.* (n.d.). Retrieved March 27, 2023, from https://www.cdc.gov/falls/hip-fractures.html

- *Mobility and Balance Loss in Seniors - Revitive.* (n.d.). Retrieved March 27, 2023, from https://www.revitive.com/us/health-center/limited-mobility-and-loss-balance-in-seniors

- Motion, B. T. (2021). Importance of Balance Training for Seniors. *Back to Motion. Denver Physical Therapy*. Retrieved March 27, 2023, from https://backtomotion.net/importance-of-balance-training-for-seniors/

Chapter 1

- *Aging changes in organs, tissue and cells: MedlinePlus Medical Encyclopedia.* (n.d.). Retrieved March 28, 2023, from https://medlineplus.gov/ency/article/004012.htm

- *Aging: What to expect.* (2022, November 3). Mayo Clinic. Retrieved March 28, 2023, from https://www.mayoclinic.org/healthy-lifestyle/healthy-aging/in-depth/aging/art-20046070

- *Bone Health and the Gut Microbiome - Today's Dietitian Magazine.* (n.d.). Retrieved March 28, 2023, from https://www.todaysdietitian.com/newarchives/0521p12.shtml
- Cscs, R. a. M. M. R. R. (2021). All About Nutrition & Bone Health. *Precision Nutrition.* Retrieved March 29, 2023, https://www.precisionnutrition.com/all-about-bone-health
- *Effects of Ageing on Joints.* (n.d.). Physiopedia. Retrieved March 29, 2023, https://www.physio-pedia.com/Effects_of_Ageing_on_Joints
- *Facts About Falls | Fall Prevention | Injury Center | CDC.* (n.d.). Retrieved March 30, 2023, from https://www.cdc.gov/falls/facts.html
- Favazzo, L., Hendesi, H., Villani, D. A., Soniwala, S., Dar, Q., Schott, E. J., Gill, S. R., & Zuscik, M. J. (2020). The gut microbiome-joint connection: implications in osteoarthritis. *Current Opinion in Rheumatology*, 32(1), 92–101. Retrieved March 30, 2023, from https://doi.org/10.1097/bor.0000000000000681
- Fox, N. (2023). The Importance of Maintaining Balance as You Age. *LHSFNA.* Retrieved March 30, 2023, from https://www.lhsfna.org/the-importance-of-maintaining-balance-as-you-age/
- Goldschmidt, V., MA. (2023). Warning: 5 Bad Things That Happen To Your Bones And Body If You Stop Exercising. *Save Our Bones.* Retrieved April 2, 2023, from https://saveourbones.com/warning-5-bad-things-that-happen-to-your-bones-and-body-if-you-stop-exercising/
- M2admin. (2022). Risks of "Sitting Disease" & Benefits of Physical Activity for Seniors. *Blakeford Senior Life.* Retrieved April 2, 2023, from https://blakeford.com/risks-of-sitting-disease-benefits-of-physical-activity-for-seniors/
- Mandel, D. (2022). The Importance of Balance as You Age. *IBX Insights.* Retrieved April 4, 2023, from https://insights.ibx.com/the-importance-of-balance-as-you-age/
- Rd, A. S. M. (2023, February 9). *The Top 10 Benefits of Regular Exercise.* Healthline. Retrieved June 14, 2023, Retrieved April 4, 2023, from https://www.healthline.com/nutrition/10-benefits-of-exercise#TOC_TITLE_HDR_2

- Skin, N. (n.d.). *What Happens When We Age and Can We Slow the Aging Process?* Nu Skin. Retrieved April 4, 2023, from https://www.nuskin.com/content/corpcom/en_US/thesource/healthandfitness/what-happens-when-we-age-and-can-we-slow-the-aging-process-.html
- *The National Council on Aging.* (n.d.). Retrieved April 4, 2023, from https://ncoa.org/article/the-life-changing-benefits-of-exercise-after-60
- *What is Two Buck Chuck? | Charles Shaw Wine | TJ Vino.* (2022, March 20). CraftJacks @ FindMeABrewery.com. Retrieved April 4, 2023, from https://www.findmeabrewery.com/two-buck-chuck/

Chapter 2

- *Posture and How It Affects Your Health | Lifespan.* (n.d.). Lifespan. Retrieved April 4, 2023, from https://www.lifespan.org/lifespan-living/posture-and-how-it-affects-your-health
- *Older Adults and Balance Problems.* (n.d.). National Institute on Aging. Retrieved April 4, 2023, from https://www.nia.nih.gov/health/older-adults-and-balance-problems
- Kutcher, M. (2022b). The Complete Guide To Great Balance For Seniors | Seniors Fitness — More Life Health - Seniors Health & Fitness. *More Life Health - Seniors Health & Fitness.* Retrieved April 5, 2023, from https://morelifehealth.com/articles/balance-guide
- Kutcher, M. (2022a). The Complete Guide To Great Balance For Seniors | Seniors Fitness — More Life Health - Seniors Health & Fitness. *More Life Health - Seniors Health & Fitness.* Retrieved April 5, 2023, from https://morelifehealth.com/articles/balance-guide
- Jones, J. F. (2021, November 22). 4 Ways to Improve Your Balance, According to a Personal Trainer. *EatingWell.* Retrieved April 5, 2023, from https://www.eatingwell.com/article/7917613/exercises-to-improve-balance/
- *How Your Posture Affects Balance - Modern Chiropractic Center.* (n.d.). Modern Chiropractic Center. Retrieved April 5, 2023, from https://modernchiropracticcenter.com/blog/how-your-posture-affects-balance/
- HealthDay. (2012, April 23). Strength Training May Give Boost to Seniors' Brains. *US News & World Report.* Retrieved April 5, 2023, from

https://health.usnews.com/health-news/news/articles/2012/04/23/strength-training-may-give-boost-to-seniors-brains

- Goldschmidt, V., MA. (2022). Reduce Your Risk Of Fracture By Improving Scores Of These Two Physical Tests. *Save Our Bones*. Retrieved April 6, 2023, from https://saveourbones.com/reduce-your-risk-of-fracture-by-improving-scores-of-these-two-physical-tests/

- Dunsky, A. (2019). The Effect of Balance and Coordination Exercises on Quality of Life in Older Adults: A Mini-Review. *Frontiers in Aging Neuroscience, 11.* Retrieved April 6, 2023, from https://doi.org/10.3389/fnagi.2019.00318

- *Care plan: Balance Impairment, Adult.* (n.d.). Retrieved April 6, 2023, from https://elsevier.health/en-US/preview/balance-impairment-cpg

- Brabaw, K., & Brabaw, K. (2021). What You Need To Know About the Connection Between Balance Training and Brain Health. *Well+Good*. Retrieved April 6, 2023, from https://www.wellandgood.com/balance-training-and-brain-health/

- *Basic Facts about Balance Problems | Aging & Health A-Z | American Geriatrics Society | HealthInAging.org.* (n.d.). Retrieved April 7, 2023, from https://www.healthinaging.org/a-z-topic/balance-problems/basic-facts

- *Balance problems - Symptoms and causes - Mayo Clinic.* (2020, June 18). Mayo Clinic. Retrieved April 7, 2023, from https://www.mayoclinic.org/diseases-conditions/balance-problems/symptoms-causes/syc-20350474

- B, B. (2021). How Your Muscles, Joints and Bones Affect Your Balance. *Heather Lane Physical Therapy*. Retrieved April 7, 2023, from https://heatherlanept.com/2021/01/06/how-your-muscles-joints-and-bones-protect-your-balance/

- Aging and Balance: Why Older People Experience Loss of Balance. (2022, July 26). *Nutrisense Journal*. Retrieved April 7, 2023, from https://www.nutrisense.io/blog/why-older-people-experience-loss-of-balance

Chapter 3

- *Why is Bone Density Important? | Summit Health.* (n.d.-a). Retrieved April 9, 2023, from https://www.summithealth.com/health-wellness/why-bone-density-important

- Waters, D., Hale, L., Grant, A., Herbison, P., & Goulding, A. (2009). Osteoporosis and gait and balance disturbances in older sarcopenic obese New Zealanders.

Osteoporosis International, 21(2), 351–357. Retrieved April 9, 2023, from https://doi.org/10.1007/s00198-009-0947-5

- *Strength training: Get stronger, leaner, healthier.* (2023, April 29). Mayo Clinic. Retrieved April 9, 2023, from https://www.mayoclinic.org/healthy-lifestyle/fitness/in-depth/strength-training/art-20046670#

- Seladi-Schulman, J., PhD. (2019, June 17). *Bone Function: Why Do We Have Bones?* Healthline. Retrieved April 11, 2023, from https://www.healthline.com/health/bone-health/bone-function#takeaway

- Rabbitt, M. (2021, November 2). 4 Best Exercises You Can Do For Strong Bones. *Prevention.* Retrieved April 11, 2023, from https://www.prevention.com/fitness/a20495708/4-best-exercises-you-can-do-for-strong-bones/

- Paddock, C., Ph.D. (2009, March 24). Scientists Find Link Between Vertigo And Osteoporosis. *Medical News Today.* Retrieved April 11, 2023, from https://www.medicalnewstoday.com/articles/143519#1

- Libretexts. (2022). 38.1: Types of Skeletal Systems - Functions of the Musculoskeletal System. *Biology LibreTexts.* Retrieved April 13, 2023, from https://bio.libretexts.org/Bookshelves/Introductory_and_General_Biology/Book%3A_General_Biology_(Boundless)/38%3A_The_Musculoskeletal_System/38.01%3A_Types_of_Skeletal_Systems_-_Functions_of_the_Musculoskeletal_System

- Kutcher, M. (2022a). The Complete Guide To Strong Bones Over 60 — More Life Health - Seniors Health & Fitness. *More Life Health - Seniors Health & Fitness.* Retrieved April 13, 2023, from https://morelifehealth.com/articles/strong-bones

- *Just Like Everything Else, Our Bones Change With Age.* (n.d.). Henry Ford Health - Detroit, MI. Retrieved April 13, 2023, from https://www.henryford.com/blog/2016/07/just-like-everything-else-our-bones-change-with-age

- Harvard Health. (2021b, October 13). *Strength training builds more than muscles.* Retrieved April 15, 2023, from https://www.health.harvard.edu/staying-healthy/strength-training-builds-more-than-muscles

- Harvard Health. (2021a, March 30). *5 ways to boost bone strength early.* Retrieved April 15, 2023, from https://www.health.harvard.edu/womens-health/5-ways-to-boost-bone-strength-early/

- Harvard Health. (2017, December 20). *How stretching keeps your joints moving*. Retrieved April 16, 2023, from https://www.health.harvard.edu/staying-healthy/how-stretching-keeps-your-joints-moving

- *10 Medications That May Increase Your Risk of Osteoporosis*. (2023, April 3). GoodRx Health. Retrieved April 16, 2023, from https://www.goodrx.com/drugs/side-effects/medications-that-may-increase-risk-for-fractures

- *Exercise and Bone Health - OrthoInfo - AAOS*. (n.d.). Retrieved April 17, 2023, from https://orthoinfo.aaos.org/en/staying-healthy/exercise-and-bone-health/

- *Calcium, Nutrition, and Bone Health - OrthoInfo - AAOS*. (n.d.). Retrieved April 17, 2023, from https://orthoinfo.aaos.org/en/staying-healthy/calcium-nutrition-and-bone-health/

- Brown, S. E. (2023). Deep breathing for bone health. *Better Bones, Better Body*. Retrieved April 17, 2023, from https://www.betterbones.com/the-natural-approach/deep-breathing-bone-health/

- Bowers, E. S. (2017, February 8). *9 Bad-for-Your-Bones Foods*. EverydayHealth.com. Retrieved April 17, 2023, from https://www.everydayhealth.com/osteoporosis-pictures/bad-for-your-bones-foods.aspx

- Bone Health and Osteoporosis Foundation. (2023, February 24). *What is osteoporosis and what causes it?* Bone Health & Osteoporosis Foundation. Retrieved April 18, 2023, from https://www.bonehealthandosteoporosis.org/patients/what-is-osteoporosis/

- *Bone Fracture Healing Supplements - Do They Work? | AlgaeCal*. (n.d.). Retrieved April 18, 2023, from https://www.algaecal.com/osteoporosis-treatment/bone-healing/

- *Bone Development & Growth | SEER Training*. (n.d.). Retrieved April 18, 2023, from https://training.seer.cancer.gov/anatomy/skeletal/growth.html

- Anderson, A. (2021, December 19). *What Are the 5 Functions of Bones?* WebMD. Retrieved April 18, 2023, from https://www.webmd.com/a-to-z-guides/what-are-five-functions-bones

Chapter 4

- Vch. (2020a). Nutrition. *International Osteoporosis Foundation*. Retrieved April 20, 2023, from https://www.osteoporosis.foundation/health-professionals/prevention/nutrition

- South-Paul, J. E. (2001, March 1). *Osteoporosis: Part I. Evaluation and Assessment.* AAFP. Retrieved April 20, 2023, from https://www.aafp.org/pubs/afp/issues/2001/0301/p897.html

- *Sally Field: An Osteoporosis Story.* (2006, April 20). WebMD. Retrieved April 20, 2023, from https://www.webmd.com/osteoporosis/features/sally-field-osteoporosis-story

- *Boniva: What if Sally Field Told The Truth?* The Save Institute. Retrieved June 19, 2023, from https://saveourbones.com/boniva-what-if-sally-field-told-the-truth/

- *Osteoporosis treatment: Medications can help.* (2022, December 6). Mayo Clinic. Retrieved April 21, 2023, from https://www.mayoclinic.org/diseases-conditions/osteoporosis/in-depth/osteoporosis-treatment/art-20046869

- *Osteoporosis Prevention: What You Need to Know.* (2008, March 24). WebMD. Retrieved April 21, 2023, from https://www.webmd.com/osteoporosis/guide/osteoporosis-prevention

- *Osteoporosis: Are You at Risk?* (1999, December 31). WebMD. Retrieved April 21, 2023, from https://www.webmd.com/osteoporosis/guide/osteoporosis-risk-factors

- *Osteoporosis.* (n.d.-a). National Institute on Aging. https://www.nia.nih.gov/health/osteoporosis

- National Library of Medicine. (n.d.). *Osteoporosis.* MedlinePlus. Retrieved April 21, 2023, from https://medlineplus.gov/osteoporosis.html

- Kutcher, M. (2022). The Complete Guide To Strong Bones Over 60 — More Life Health - Seniors Health & Fitness. *More Life Health - Seniors Health & Fitness.* Retrieved April 22, 2023, from https://morelifehealth.com/articles/strong-bones#3g

- Geng, C. (2021, November 30). *What is secondary osteoporosis?* Retrieved April 22, 2023, from https://www.medicalnewstoday.com/articles/secondary-osteoporosis#primary-vs-secondary

- Department of Health & Human Services. (n.d.). *Osteoporosis.* Better Health Channel. Retrieved April 22, 2023, from https://www.betterhealth.vic.gov.au/health/conditionsandtreatments/osteoporosis

- CBS Detroit. (2011, April 7). Michigan Tech Studying Bears To Beat Osteoporosis. *CBS News*. Retrieved April 22, 2023, from https://www.cbsnews.com/detroit/news/michigan-tech-studying-bears-to-beat-osteoporosis/

- Bone Health and Osteoporosis Foundation. (2023, March 15). *Osteoporosis Diet & Nutrition: Foods for Bone Health*. Bone Health & Osteoporosis Foundation. Retrieved April 22, 2023, from https://www.bonehealthandosteoporosis.org/patients/treatment/nutrition/

- Bone Health and Osteoporosis Foundation. (2022, December 15). *Bone Density Test, Osteoporosis Screening & T-score Interpretation*. Bone Health & Osteoporosis Foundation. Retrieved April 23, 2023, from https://www.bonehealthandosteoporosis.org/patients/diagnosis-information/bone-density-examtesting/

Chapter 5

- Zafar, H., Albarrati, A., Alghadir, A. H., & Iqbal, Z. A. (2018). Effect of Different Head-Neck Postures on the Respiratory Function in Healthy Males. *BioMed Research International, 2018*, 1–4. Retrieved April 26, 2023, from https://doi.org/10.1155/2018/4518269

- Trc. (2021, September 2). Osteopathy: How Bad Posture affects your Breathing. *theroundclinic*. Retrieved April 26, 2023, from https://www.theroundclinic.com/single-post/osteopathy-how-bad-posture-affects-your-breathing

- *Stretching: Focus on flexibility*. (2022, February 12). Mayo Clinic. Retrieved April 26, 2023, from https://www.mayoclinic.org/healthy-lifestyle/fitness/in-depth/stretching/art-20047931

- Reports, C. (2018, December 3). Straight facts about improving your posture. *Washington Post*. Retrieved April 26, 2023, from https://www.washingtonpost.com/national/health-science/straight-facts-about-improving-your-posture/2018/11/30/db4e4ac0-f1ad-11e8-80d0-f7e1948d55f4_story.html

- Reference, M. T. (2017, August 3). *Postural Assessment (Visual Observation)*. Medical Massage Therapy. Retrieved April 27, 2023, from https://www.massagetherapyreference.com/postural-assessment/

- *Posture*. (n.d.). Physiopedia. https://www.physio-pedia.com/Posture
- National Library of Medicine. (n.d.-c). *Guide to Good Posture*. Retrieved April 27, 2023, from https://medlineplus.gov/guidetogoodposture.html
- National Library of Medicine. (n.d.-b). *Guide to Good Posture*. Retrieved April 27, 2023, from https://medlineplus.gov/guidetogoodposture.html
- National Library of Medicine. (n.d.-a). *Guide to Good Posture*. Retrieved April 27, 2023, from https://medlineplus.gov/guidetogoodposture.html#:~:text=Posture%20is%20how%20you%20hold,sitting%2C%20standing%2C%20or%20sleeping
- Nagymáté, G., Takács, M., & Kiss, R. M. (2018). Does bad posture affect the standing balance? *Cogent Medicine*, *5*(1), 1503778. Retrieved April 27, 2023, from https://doi.org/10.1080/2331205x.2018.1503778
- Mayer, B. A. (2022, August 4). Stretching May Help Slow Cognitive Decline as Well as Aerobic Exercise. *Healthline*. Retrieved April 28, 2023, from https://www.healthline.com/health-news/stretching-may-help-slow-cognitive-decline-as-well-as-aerobic-exercise
- Institute for Quality and Efficiency in Health Care (IQWiG). (2018, July 12). *How do joints work?* InformedHealth.org - NCBI Bookshelf. Retrieved April 28, 2023, from https://www.ncbi.nlm.nih.gov/books/NBK279363/
- *How Your Posture Affects Balance - Modern Chiropractic Center*. (n.d.). Modern Chiropractic Center. Retrieved April 28, 2023, from https://modernchiropracticcenter.com/blog/how-your-posture-affects-balance/
- Here's *What Happens When You Have Bad Posture: iMed Regeneration Center: Integrative Medical Clinics*. (n.d.). Retrieved April 28, 2023, from https://www.imedregeneration.com/blog/heres-what-happens-when-you-have-bad-posture
- Healthdirect Australia. (n.d.). *Bones, muscles and joints*. Healthdirect. Retrieved April 29, 2023, from https://www.healthdirect.gov.au/bones-muscles-and-joints
- Harvard Health. (2017, December 20). *How stretching keeps your joints moving*. Retrieved April 29, 2023, from https://www.health.harvard.edu/staying-healthy/how-stretching-keeps-your-joints-moving

- *Get fit at home with this 10-minute resistance band workout.* (2022, January 14). [Video]. TODAY.com. Retrieved April 29, 2023, from https://www.today.com/health/diet-fitness/posture-exercises-rcna12220
- Garrett, M. (n.d.). *Senior Fitness: Importance of good posture.* Retrieved April 26, 2023, from https://wellness.nifs.org/blog/bid/81663/Senior-Fitness-Importance-of-good-posture
- Dalton, S. (2020, August 18). *Breathe Deeper to Improve Health and Posture.* Healthline. Retrieved April 29, 2023, from https://www.healthline.com/health/breathe-deeper-improve-health-and-posture
- Becki, A., & Becki, A. (2021, December 16). Stretching Is Increasingly Important with Age. *Fitness Nation.* Retrieved April 30, 2023, from https://fitness-nation.net/2021/07/07/stretching-is-increasingly-important-with-age/
- Bataineh, A., MD. (2021, December 14). Why we lose flexibility with age and what to do about it. *Span Health.* Retrieved April 30, 2023, from https://www.span.health/blog/why-we-lose-flexibility-with-age-and-what-to-do-about-it
- Andrewlouder. (2018, December 10). *5 Benefits of Stretching | Preferred Physical Therapy.* Retrieved April 30, 2023, from Preferred Physical Therapy. https://preferredptkc.com/2018/12/5-benefits-of-stretching

Chapter 6

- Tulloch, A. (2021, February 19). Diagnosed with Osteoporosis at 18 years of age - Bobby Clay's warning to other athletes. *Olympics.com.* Retrieved May 1, 2023, from https://olympics.com/en/news/diagnosed-with-osteoporosis-at-18-years-old-bobby-clay-s-warning-to-other-athlet
- Palacios, C. (2006b). The Role of Nutrients in Bone Health, from A to Z. *Critical Reviews in Food Science and Nutrition,* 46(8), 621–628. Retrieved May 1, 2023, from https://doi.org/10.1080/10408390500466174
- Palacios, C. (2006a). The Role of Nutrients in Bone Health, from A to Z. *Critical Reviews in Food Science and Nutrition,* 46(8), 621–628. Retrieved May 1, 2023, from https://doi.org/10.1080/10408390500466174
- *Osteoporosis Diet & Nutrition: Foods to Eat & Avoid | AlgaeCal.* (n.d.). Retrieved May 1, 2023, from https://www.algaecal.com/osteoporosis-treatment/diet/

- Lewis, J. R., Voortman, T., & Ioannidis, J. P. A. (2021). Evaluating and Strengthening the Evidence for Nutritional Bone Research: Ready to Break New Ground? *Journal of Bone and Mineral Research, 36*(2), 219–226. Retrieved May 1, 2023, from https://doi.org/10.1002/jbmr.4236

- Kutcher, M. (2022c). HOW TO EAT FOR STRONGER BONES - THE COMPLETE GUIDE — More Life Health - Seniors Health & Fitness. *More Life Health - Seniors Health & Fitness.* Retrieved May 2, 2023, from https://morelifehealth.com/articles/strong-bones-part2#5a

- Kutcher, M. (2022b). HOW TO EAT FOR STRONGER BONES - THE COMPLETE GUIDE — More Life Health - Seniors Health & Fitness. *More Life Health - Seniors Health & Fitness.* Retrieved May 2, 2023, from https://morelifehealth.com/articles/strong-bones-part2#2d

- Kutcher, M. (2022a). HOW TO EAT FOR STRONGER BONES - THE COMPLETE GUIDE — More Life Health - Seniors Health & Fitness. *More Life Health - Seniors Health & Fitness.* Retrieved May 3, 2023, from https://morelifehealth.com/articles/strong-bones-part2#2b

- Karpouzos, A., Diamantis, E., Farmaki, P., Savvanis, S., & Troupis, T. (2017). Nutritional Aspects of Bone Health and Fracture Healing. *Journal of Osteoporosis, 2017,* 1–10. https://pubmed.ncbi.nlm.nih.gov/16080661/https://doi.org/10.1155/2017/4218472

- Goldschmidt, V., MA. (2023). Two Studies Show That Coconut Oil Prevents Bone Loss. *Save Our Bones.* https://saveourbones.com/two-studies-show-that-coconut-oil-prevents-bone-loss/

- Goldschmidt, V., MA. (2022c). Why You Should Be Eating Blackberries. Hint: They're Among The Richest Source Of These Bone-Protective Nutrients. *Save Our Bones.* Retrieved May 3, 2023, from https://saveourbones.com/why-you-should-be-eating-blackberries-hint-theyre-among-the-richest-source-of-these-bone-protective-nutrients/

- Goldschmidt, V., MA. (2022b). The Top 13 Most Hydrating Foods Your Bones Crave. *Save Our Bones.* Retrieved May 3, 2023, from https://saveourbones.com/the-top-13-most-hydrating-foods-your-bones-crave/

- Goldschmidt, V., MA. (2022a). 9 Easy Tricks To Drink More Water… And Nourish Your Bones. *Save Our Bones*. Retrieved May 4, 2023, from https://saveourbones.com/9-easy-tricks-to-drink-more-water-and-nourish-your-bones/

- Goldschmidt, V., MA. (2016). 5 Foods That Naturally Improve Your Balance. *Save Our Bones*. https://saveourbones.com/5-foods-that-improve-balance/

- Fasihi, S., Fazelian, S., Farahbod, F., Moradi, F., & Dehghan, M. (2021). Effect of Alkaline Drinking Water on Bone Density of Postmenopausal Women with Osteoporosis. *Journal of Menopausal Medicine, 27*(2), 94. Retrieved May 3, 2023, from https://doi.org/10.6118/jmm.20036

- [Diet, nutrition and bone health]. (2005, April 1). PubMed. Retrieved May 3, 2023, from https://pubmed.ncbi.nlm.nih.gov/16080661/

- Bueno, S. (2021, August 10). *How Proper Hydration Affects Bone Health - Watauga Orthopaedics*. Watauga Orthopaedics. Retrieved May 4, 2023, from https://www.wataugaortho.com/2018/04/20/how-proper-hydration-affects-bone-health/

- BoneCoach. (2022, November 19). *Is Bone Broth Good For Bone Health? (What The Research Says) BoneCoachTM - Stronger Bones. Active Future*. BoneCoachTM - Stronger Bones. Active Future. Retrieved May 5, 2023, from https://bonecoach.com/is-bone-broth-good-for-bone-health/

- *Bone Health and the Gut Microbiome - Today's Dietitian Magazine*. (n.d.). Retrieved May 1, 2023, from https://www.todaysdietitian.com/newarchives/0521p12.shtml

- *Bone Health | Nutrition for Healthy Bones | Alleviate Neck or Back Pain*. (2023, February 2). National Spine Health Foundation. Retrieved May 5, 2023, from https://spinehealth.org/article/lifelong-nutrition-for-healthy-bones/

- Balance & Dizziness Canada. (2022, July 4). *Eating Well - Balance & Dizziness Canada*. Balance & Dizziness Canada - Supporting, Inspiring and Educating Those Affected by Balance and Dizziness Disorders. Retrieved May 5, 2023, from https://balanceanddizziness.org/help-yourself/eating-well/

- Bailey, R. L., Sahni, S., Chocano-Bedoya, P. O., Daly, R. M., Welch, A. A., Bischoff-Ferrari, H. A., & Weaver, C. M. (2019). Best Practices for Conducting Observational Research to Assess the Relation between Nutrition and Bone: An

International Working Group Summary. *Advances in Nutrition, 10*(3), 391–409. Retrieved May 5, 2023, from https://doi.org/10.1093/advances/nmy111

- EWG Science Team. (2023, March 15). EWG's 2023 Shopper's Guide to Pesticides in Produce. Retrieved June 20, 2023, from https://www.ewg.org/foodnews/summary.php
- Fishman, Loren, MD. (2017). *What is Astaxanthin?* AlgaeCal. Retrieved June 20, 2023, from https://blog.algaecal.com/astaxanthin/

Chapter 7

- And1general. (2022). The Importance of Accountability in Your Fitness Journey. *1AND1.* Retrieved May 7, 2023, from https://www.1and1life.com/blog/fitness-journey/
- Audrey. (2021). The Benefits of Proper Form When Exercising: Do You Have Correct Gym Form? *Jack City Fitness.* Retrieved May 7, 2023, from https://jackcityfitness.com/why-having-proper-fitness-form-technique-is-important/#
- Department of Health & Human Services. (n.d.). *Exercise - the low-down on hydration.* Better Health Channel. Retrieved May 7, 2023, from https://www.betterhealth.vic.gov.au/health/healthyliving/Exercise-the-low-down-on-water-and-drinks
- Diane Rellinger, Michigan State University Extension. (2016). Regular breathing and proper posture when exercising is important. *MSU Extension.* Retrieved May 7, 2023, from https://www.canr.msu.edu/news/regular_breathing_and_proper_posture_when_exercising_is_important
- Duncan, C. (n.d.). 10 Things That Steal Our Motivation—and How to Get It Back. *Shine.* Retrieved May 8, 2023, from https://advice.theshineapp.com/articles/10-things-that-steal-our-motivation-and-how-to-get-it-back/
- Harvard Health. (2017, January 24). *Why good posture matters.* Retrieved May 8, 2023, from https://www.health.harvard.edu/staying-healthy/why-good-posture-matters
- Healthdirect Australia. (n.d.). *Motivation: How to get started and stay motivated.* Healthdirect. Retrieved May 8, 2023, from

https://www.healthdirect.gov.au/motivation-how-to-get-started-and-staying-motivated

- MS, S. P. E. (2023). How to Breathe Properly During Your Workout. *The Perfect Workout*. Retrieved May 8, 2023, from
  https://www.theperfectworkout.com/breathe-properly-during-workout/

- MSc, L. R. (2023). The Importance, Benefits, and Value of Goal Setting. *PositivePsychology.com*. Retrieved May 8, 2023, from
  https://positivepsychology.com/benefits-goal-setting/#:~:text=Setting%20goals%20can%20help%20us,we%20truly%20want%20in%20life.

- *Set your goals and make them happen.* (n.d.). Action for Happiness. Retrieved May 8, 2023, from https://actionforhappiness.org/take-action/set-your-goals-and-make-them-happen

- Taylor, K. (2022, October 3). *Adult Dehydration*. StatPearls - NCBI Bookshelf. Retrieved May 10, 2023, from
  https://www.ncbi.nlm.nih.gov/books/NBK555956/

- *The National Council on Aging.* (n.d.-a). Retrieved May 10, 2023, from
  https://www.ncoa.org/article/how-to-stay-hydrated-for-better-health

- Voropay, E. (2016). Visualization Techniques – Mental Tips for Better Workouts. *ShapeFit.com*. Retrieved May 12, 2023, from
  https://www.shapefit.com/exercise/visualization-techniques-workouts.html

- *Why is hydration important during exercise?* (n.d.). Hydrant. Retrieved May 12, 2023, from https://www.drinkhydrant.com/blogs/news/hydration-and-exercise

Made in the USA
Las Vegas, NV
29 December 2023